A Basic Guide to Understanding, Assessing, and Teaching Phonological Awareness

Joseph K. Torgesen
Patricia G. Mathes

pro·ed
An International Publisher

8700 Shoal Creek Boulevard
Austin, Texas 78757-6897
800/897-3202   Fax 800/397-7633
Order online at http://www.proedinc.com

© 2000 by PRO-ED, Inc.
8700 Shoal Creek Boulevard
Austin, Texas 78757-6897
800/897-3202   Fax 800/397-7633
Order online at http://www.proedinc.com

Library of Congress Cataloging-in-Publication Data

Torgesen, Joseph K.
    A basic guide to understanding, assessing, and teaching phonological awareness /
Joseph K. Torgesen, Patricia G. Mathes.
        p.   cm.
    Includes bibliographical references.
    ISBN 0-89079-844-3 (softcover : alk. paper)
    1. Children—Language.   2. English language—Phonetics—Study and teaching (Early
childhood)   3. Reading—Phonetic method.   4. Language awareness in children.   I. Mathes,
Patricia G.   II. Title.
LB1139.L3 .T64   2000
372.46'5 2 21
                                                                99-045546
                                                                CIP

This book is designed in Goudy.

Production Director: Alan Grimes
Production Coordinator: Karen Swain
Managing Editor: Chris Olson
Art Director: Thomas Barkley
Designer: Jason Crosier
Print Buyer: Alicia Woods
Preproduction Coordinator: Chris Anne Worsham
Assistant Managing Editor: Martin Wilson
Project Editor: Debra Berman
Publishing Assistant: Jason Morris

Printed in the United States of America

1   2   3   4   5   6   7   8   9   10   04   03   02   01   00

CONTENTS

PREFACE

A Basic Guide to Understanding, Assessing, and Teaching Phonological Awareness was prepared as a resource to help teachers discover ways to incorporate instruction about phonological awareness into their prereading and reading curriculum. The development of this manual was partially supported by a grant from the State of Florida Department of Education, and it is designed to be of direct assistance to teachers and administrators in selecting curriculum materials to train teachers in assessing the development of phonemic awareness.

The discovery of the importance of phonemic awareness in early reading is one of the most important breakthroughs in reading instruction in the last 20 years. Research now shows very clearly that at least 20% of school children will experience difficulties learning to read without explicit instruction to stimulate phonological awareness. Such instruction also appears to accelerate reading development in all children. *It is essential that all teachers who work with young children, as well as those who work with children experiencing problems learning to read, understand what phonological awareness is, how it can be quickly assessed, and how to help children acquire it.*

This manual is divided into three sections. The first section describes what phonological awareness is and how it is related to reading instruction; the second section presents information about the assessment of phonological awareness; and the third section describes how instruction in phonological awareness can be integrated into reading instruction. The last two sections present detailed information and evaluations of presently available tests and curriculum materials in this area.

We hope teachers will find this manual useful in their efforts to help all children acquire effective literacy skills. We are convinced that information about phonological awareness can make a difference if it is understood and applied properly.

SECTION

What Phonological Awareness Is and Why It Is Important in Reading

Phonological awareness has become one of the most important educational buzz-words of the 1990s. Teachers are talking about it, parents are trying to understand it, and publishers of early reading materials are trying to include it. However, it is a concept that is easily misunderstood. Some confuse it with phonics and others consider it to be a part of general print awareness, yet it is neither of these things. Teachers must be careful about how they teach it to children; unless teachers thoroughly understand the concept and its role in reading development, they may easily teach it in ways that produce little benefit to children. In this introductory section, we attempt to share what is currently known about the nature of phonological awareness, why it is important in reading growth, why children differ from one another in their ability to acquire it, and how teachers may most effectively incorporate it into reading instruction. Although we currently know a great deal about this concept, there is still much that is not known, so we shall try to point out some of the questions along the way.

What Is Phonological Awareness?

To understand the concept of phonological awareness, one must first know what a phoneme is. A phoneme is the smallest unit of sound in a language that makes a difference to its meaning. For example, the word *cat* has three

1

phonemes, /k/- /a/- /t/. One can produce the word *bat* by changing the first phoneme, the word *cot* by changing the second phoneme, and the word *cab* by altering the final phoneme. Words in English (in fact, in all languages) are composed of strings of phonemes, allowing speakers of English to create all the words they will ever need by using various combinations of only 44 different speech sounds.

Speech scientists have discovered that the human brain is specifically adapted for processing many different kinds of linguistic information, and one part of that biological endowment allows humans to process the complex phonological information in speech without actually being aware of the individual phonemes themselves. This is one of the human abilities that allows speech to be acquired in a natural process, so that almost everyone in the world learns to speak a language with very little direct instruction. However, because phonemes are represented by letters in print, learning to read requires that children become consciously aware of phonemes as individual segments in words. In fact, phonological awareness is most commonly defined as one's sensitivity to, or explicit awareness of, the phonological structure of words in one's language. In short, it involves the ability to notice, think about, or manipulate the individual sounds in words.

One of the early signs of emerging sensitivity to the phonological structure of words is the ability to play rhyming games and activities. To determine whether two words rhyme, the child must attend to the sounds in words rather than their meanings. In addition, the child must focus attention on only one *part* of a word rather than the way it sounds as a whole. As children grow in awareness of the phonemes in words, they become able to judge whether words have the same first or last sounds, and with further development, they become able to actually isolate and pronounce the first, last, or middle sounds in words. At its highest levels of development, awareness of individual phonemes in words is shown by the ability to separately pronounce the sounds in even multisyllable words, or to tell exactly how two words like *task* and *tacks* are different (the order of the last two phonemes is reversed).

Acquiring phonological awareness actually involves learning two kinds of things about language. First, it involves learning that words can be divided into segments of sound smaller than a syllable. Second, it involves learning about individual phonemes themselves. As children acquire more and more conscious knowledge of the distinctive features of phonemes (how they sound when they occur in words, or how they feel when they are pronounced), they become more adept at noticing their identity and order when they occur in words. For example, while children in the first semester of first grade might be able to isolate and identify the first or last sound of a word such as *man*, by the end of first grade, most children can easily, and relatively automatically, segment all the sounds in a more complex word such as *clap*.

Why Is Phonological Awareness Important in Learning To Read?

Phonological awareness is important because it is necessary for understanding how words in our language are represented in print. When children learn to read, they must acquire two different kinds of skills: how to identify printed words and how to comprehend written material. Their major challenge when they first enter school is to learn to accurately identify printed words, and this brings them face to face with the alphabetic principle. English is an alphabetic language, meaning that words are represented in print roughly at the level of phonemes. For example, the word *cat* has three phonemes, and three letters are used to represent them; the word *which* also has three phonemes, but five letters are used to represent them.

In English, the alphabetic principle presents two important learning challenges to children. First, individual phonemes are not readily apparent as individual segments in normal speech. When we hear the word *dog*, for example, the phonemes overlap with one another (they are coarticulated) so that we hear a single burst of sound rather than three individual segments. Coarticulating the phonemes in words (e.g., starting to pronounce the second phoneme /r/ in the word *frost* while still saying the first phoneme /f/) makes speech fluent, but it also makes it hard for many children to become aware of phonemes as individual segments of sound within words.

The second challenge presented by the alphabetic principle in English is that there is not always a regular one-to-one correspondence between letters and phonemes. For example, some phonemes are represented by more than one letter (e.g., *ch*, *sh*, *wh*, *ai*, *oi*). In addition, sometimes the phoneme represented by a letter changes, depending on other letters in the word (*not* vs. *note*, *fit* vs. *fight*, *not* vs. *notion*), or pronunciation of parts of some words may not follow any regular letter–phoneme correspondence patterns (e.g., *yacht* or *choir*).

If understanding and using the alphabetic principle in reading words presents such learning challenges for children, the obvious question, and one that has been repeatedly asked over the last century, is whether it is really necessary for children to understand the principle and master its use in order to become good readers. On the basis of research on reading, reading development, and reading instruction conducted over the past 20 years, researchers now know that the answer to this question is very strongly in the affirmative (Beck & Juel, 1995). Children who quickly come to understand the relationships between letters and phonemes, and who learn to use this information as an aid to identifying words in print almost invariably become better readers than children who have difficulty acquiring these skills (Share & Stanovich, 1995).

There are at least three ways in which phonological awareness is important in acquiring accurate word reading skills.

▶ 1. *Phonological awareness helps children understand the alphabetic principle.* Without at least a beginning level of phonological awareness, children have no way of understanding how the words from their oral language are represented in print. Unless they understand that words have sound segments at the level of the phoneme, they cannot take advantage of an alphabetic script (Liberman, Shankweiler, & Liberman, 1989). They also will not be able to understand the rationale for learning individual letter sounds, and the common strategy of sounding out words in beginning reading will not make sense to them.

2. *Phonological awareness helps children notice the regular ways that letters represent sounds in words.* If children can notice all four phonemes in the spoken word *flat*, it helps them understand the way the letters in the written word correspond to the sounds. This ability to notice the match between the letters and sounds in words has two potential benefits to children learning to read. First, it reinforces knowledge of individual letter–sound correspondences, and second, it helps in forming strong memories of whole words so they can be accurately recognized when they are encountered in print again. Research has shown that the associations children form between *all* the letters and *all* the sounds in words creates the kind of "sight word" representations that are the basis of fluent reading (Ehri, 1998).

3. *Phonological awareness makes it possible to generate possibilities for words in context that are only partially sounded out.* For example, consider a first-grade child who encounters a sentence such as "John's father put his bicycle in the car," and cannot recognize the fifth word. A relatively early level of phonological awareness supports the ability to search one's mental dictionary for words that begin with similar sounds. Thus, if the child knows the sound represented by the letter 'b', he or she can mentally search for words that begin with that sound and fit the context. As children acquire more

knowledge of phonics and can sound out more letters in words, their search for words with similar phonemes in them can proceed much more quickly and accurately.

As should be clear from this analysis, phonemic awareness has its primary impact on reading growth through its effect on children's ability to phonemically decode words in text. Although phonemic decoding skills should never be considered the end goal of reading, research now shows that, for most children, these skills are a critical step along the way toward effective reading skills.

To illustrate concretely the impact that deficient phonological awareness can have on the growth of reading skills, the graph in Figure 1.1 presents information on the growth of word reading ability in two groups of children who began first grade with different levels of phonological awareness. One of the groups of children, in the sample of 200 children, began first grade in the bottom 20% on measures on phonological awareness, and the other group consisted of everyone scoring above the 20th percentile (Torgesen, Wagner, & Rashotte, 1994). All children had general verbal ability in the normal range. The numbers at the right of the graphs represent average grade level scores at the end of fifth grade for these children.

The top panel of Figure 1.1 shows that children with weak phonological awareness ended up about two grade levels below their peers in sight word reading ability, and the bottom panel shows that their phonemic decoding skills were more than 3 grade levels below their peers. On a measure of reading comprehension, the children with weak phonological awareness obtained a grade score of 3.9, which was 3 years behind the score of 6.9 obtained by their peers.

It is important to remember that phonological awareness is not the only knowledge or skill required to learn to read. Longitudinal research has shown that phonological awareness is *necessary but not sufficient* for becoming a good reader. Other phonological abilities may also affect children's ability to acquire phonemic decoding ability and sight word fluency, and a good vocabulary, general knowledge about the world, good thinking skills, and an interest in reading are clearly important in the development of reading comprehension.

What Is the Normal Developmental Course for Phonological Awareness?

Although reliable information about normal growth rates in phonological awareness is one of the questions remaining for further research, it is possible to

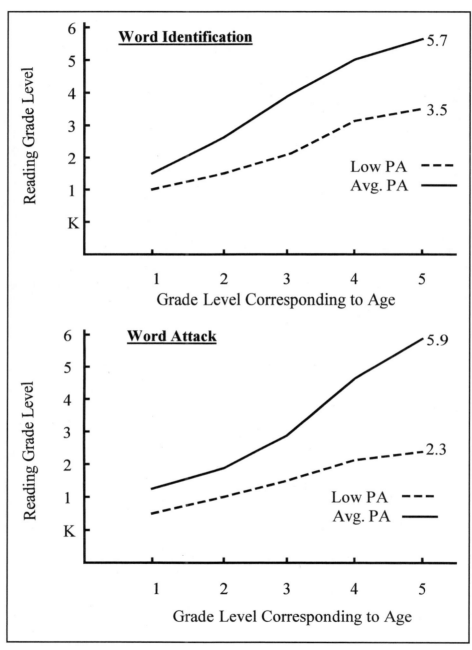

Figure 1.1. Growth of sight word (word identification) and phonemic decoding (word attack) skills in children who begin first grade above (avg.) or below the 20th percentile in phonological awareness (PA).

outline some broad benchmarks of development for the early school years. In looking at Table 1.1, it is important to remember that these are all oral language tasks. Phonological awareness is an *oral language* skill, and a child does not have to have any knowledge of letters to demonstrate beginning levels of phonological awareness. In contrast, the *phonics skills* that are actually used in reading require children to know the ways that letters represent the sounds in *printed* words. "Average" development may vary across school districts, and phonological awareness at school entry varies substantially in children from different kinds of home and cultural backgrounds. Nevertheless, children who fall very far below the rate of development outlined in Table 1.1 are likely to experience difficulties acquiring early reading skills.

A few recent research studies have found that children may begin to develop early forms of phonological awareness as young as 2½ to 3 years of age (e.g., Lonigan, Burgess, Anthony, & Barker, 1998). However, it is important to recognize that when we speak of phonological awareness in children as young as 3 years old, we are speaking of a very different level of this ability than is shown by most first-grade children. The tasks used with very young children typically assess sensitivity to syllables and rhyme, which are more

Table 1.1
Benchmarks of Normal Development in Phonological Awareness

Grade Level	Average Child's Ability
Beginning Kindergarten	Can tell whether two words rhyme
	Can generate a rhyme for a simple word (e.g., *cat* or *dot*)
	Or can be easily taught to do these tasks
End of Kindergarten	Can isolate and pronounce the beginning sound in a word (e.g., /n / in *nose* or /f / in *fudge*)
	Can blend the sounds in two phoneme words [e.g., *boy* (/b/-/oi/) or *me* (/m/-/e/)]
Midway through First Grade	Can isolate and pronounce all the sounds in two- and three-phoneme words
	Can blend the sounds in four-phoneme words containing initial consonant blends
End of First Grade	Can isolate and pronounce the sounds in four-phoneme words containing initial blends
	Can blend the sounds in four- and five-phoneme words containing initial and final blends

global aspects of the phonological structure of words than are phonemes. These measures assess general *phonological awareness* rather than *phonemic awareness*. The term phonological awareness, thus, has a slightly different meaning from the term phonemic awareness, although these terms are frequently used interchangeably. The former term is more general and encompassing, and can be used when referring to all levels of awareness of the phonological structure of words. The latter term is frequently used to describe tasks or instructional activities that are focused specifically on the individual phonemes in words. In this manual, we usually use the term phonological awareness because it is more general, but often we are referring to awareness at the level of the phoneme. The distinction between general phonological awareness and more specific phoneme awareness is actually an important one because tasks that assess a more global level of phonological sensitivity (e.g., awareness of syllables or sensitivity to rhyme) are not as predictive of reading growth as measures that specifically assess awareness or sensitivity to individual phonemes in words (Hoien, Lundberg, Stanovich, & Bjaalid, 1995).

What Causes Differences Among Children in Phonological Awareness?

When children enter school, there is substantial variability in their level of phonological awareness, and their response to instruction in kindergarten produces an even larger range of individual differences by the end of the school year. The factors that cause individual differences among children in phonological awareness when they enter school are genetic endowment and preschool linguistic experience.

Research conducted over the last 20 years has shown that children vary significantly "in the phonological component of their natural capacity for language" (Liberman et al., 1989, p. 17). This phonological ability, or talent, is a strongly heritable trait. In other words, children can vary in their talent for processing the phonological features of language in the same way that they vary among one another in musical ability, height, or hair color. In fact, large-scale studies involving identical twins have shown that about half of all the variation in linguistically related phonological skills is inherited (Olson, Forsberg, Wise, & Rack, 1994).

Talent in the area of phonological processing can vary quite independently from other areas of intellectual ability, although many studies show that it is at least moderately correlated with general learning ability (Wagner, Torgesen, Laughon, Simmons, & Rashotte, 1993). It is possible, for example, to be average or above average in general intelligence while being severely deficient in the ability to acquire phonological awareness. Sometimes a lack of talent for processing the phonological features of language produces noticeable effects on language and speech development prior to school entry, but frequently it does not. In other words, it is possible to have a lack of talent in the area of phonological processing that does not affect the ability to become a good speaker or hearer of one's native language, but that does affect early reading development. The reason for this is that reading requires children to become consciously aware of the phonemic segments in words whereas speech does not.

The child's preschool linguistic environment can also exert a strong influence on sensitivity to the phonological structure of words at the time of school entry (Whitehurst & Lonigan, 1998). Early experience with nursery rhymes, for example, can help children begin to notice and think about the phonological structure of words. Several research studies have shown that children who know more about nursery rhymes at age 3 are those who tend to be more highly developed in general phonological awareness at age 4, and in phonemic awareness at age 6 (Bryant, MacLean, Bradley, & Crossland, 1990). Some recent work has begun to verify that children who come from backgrounds in which they have been more frequently exposed to letters and their names, and to various kinds of reading activities, show more advanced phonological awareness upon school entry than those with less experience in these areas (Whitehurst & Lonigan, 1998).

After children enter school, the growth of their phonological awareness depends not only on what they are taught, but also on their response to that instruction. Reading programs that contain explicit phonics instruction produce more rapid growth in phonological awareness than approaches that do not provide direct instruction in this area (Foorman, Francis, Fletcher, Schatschneider, & Mehta, 1998). In addition, children who respond well to early reading instruction grow much more rapidly in phonological awareness than those who experience difficulties learning early reading skills. In this sense, phonological awareness is both a *cause* and a *consequence* of differences among children in the rate at which they learn to read. Those who begin reading instruction with sufficiently developed phonological awareness understand the instruction better, master the alphabetic principle faster, and learn to read quite readily. In contrast, those who enter first grade with weak phonological awareness do not respond well to early reading instruction and thus do not have the learning experiences or acquire the reading knowledge and skill that stimulate further growth and refinement of phonological awareness.

Can Direct Instruction in Phonological Awareness Help Children Learn To Read More Easily?

Many research studies have shown that it is possible to stimulate growth in phonological awareness by explicit instruction (Ball & Blachman, 1991; Lundberg, Frost, & Peterson, 1988). Research has also shown that the effectiveness of oral language training in phonological awareness is significantly improved if, at some point in the training, children are helped to apply their newly acquired phonological awareness directly to very simple reading and spelling tasks (Bradley & Bryant, 1985). For example, children who have been taught a few letter sounds, and who have achieved a beginning level of phonemic awareness, should be able to identify the first letter of a word when they hear it pronounced. They might also be led to substitute different letters at the beginning of a word such as *cat* to make different words. They could also be asked to pronounce the "sounds" of the letters 'a' and 't', and then blend them together to form a word.

Most instructional programs in phonemic awareness begin with oral language activities. However, most also conclude by leading children to apply to reading and spelling activities their newly acquired ability to think about the phonemic segments in words. *This is a very important point.* Stimulation of phonological awareness should never be considered an isolated instructional end in itself. It will be most useful as part of the reading curriculum if it is blended seamlessly with instruction and experiences using letter–sound correspondences to read and spell words.

Recent research indicates that instructional programs in this area must go beyond the very beginning levels of general phonological awareness to activities that draw attention to the phonemes in words. Thus, programs that teach only rhyme or syllable awareness will not be as effective as those that help children to become aware of individual phonemes in words (Hoien et al., 1995).

Unfortunately, it is in the area of instruction in phonological awareness that many important questions remain unanswered (Blachman, 1997). This, of course, does not mean that teachers should delay implementing what is known, but rather that they should be open to refinements in the knowledge in this area as research progresses. For example, researchers do not yet have specific information, beyond the simple distinction already made, about how much phonological awareness is optimal for beginning reading instruction. One might think, "the more the merrier," but concentrating on developing more phonological awareness than is needed before beginning actual instruction in reading may be a waste of valuable instructional time. Further, it is not yet clear what the optimal combination of training tasks might be. Although training using oral language activities can stimulate the growth of phonological awareness, direct instruction in phonics and spelling can also produce development in this area.

Another important question is whether training in phonological awareness prior to the beginning of reading instruction can actually prevent serious reading disabilities. Classroom-level or small group training in phonological awareness consistently produces improvements in reading growth for groups of children. However, in all studies conducted thus far, a large range of individual differences has been demonstrated in response to the instruction, with the most phonologically impaired children showing the least growth in response to small group or classroom-level instruction (Torgesen & Davis, 1996).

It is likely that classroom-level instruction in phonological awareness, by itself, will not be sufficient to prevent reading disabilities in children who have serious deficiencies in phonological processing (Torgesen, in press). These children will require more intensive, detailed, and explicit instruction to achieve the levels of phonemic awareness required to support good reading growth. One program that has been used successfully to stimulate phonological awareness in children and adults with severe reading impairments actually helps them to discover the mouth movements or articulatory gestures that are associated with each phoneme (P. Lindamood & P. Lindamood, 1998). One of the goals of this method of instruction is to provide a way for individuals to "feel" the sounds in words as well as hear them.

On the basis of substantial and consistent research findings, it is clear at this point that high-quality instruction to enhance phonological awareness should be part of reading instruction for every child. This instruction will accelerate the reading growth of all children, and it appears vital for at least 20% of children to acquire useful reading skills. However, it is also clear that this instruction is only one small part of an effective overall reading curriculum. Good training in phonological awareness should be combined with systematic, direct, and explicit instruction in phonics, as well as rich experiences with language and literature, to make a strong early reading curriculum. This "balanced" reading curriculum should also include early and consistent experiences with writing, as a means both to help children learn more about the alphabetic principle and to enhance their awareness of reading and writing as meaningful activities. Of course, all this instruction should be provided within a supportive, rewarding context that provides instructional adjustments for children depending on the different ways they respond to the basic reading curriculum.

S E C T I O N

ASSESSMENT OF PHONOLOGICAL AWARENESS

The primary purpose for the assessment of phonological awareness is to identify children who may require extra instructional help. Although phonological awareness can be effectively stimulated by group activities at the classroom level, there will always be a proportion of children who need more intensive, or more explicit, instruction to achieve adequate growth in this area. In the first part of this section, we present some general issues involved in selecting and using measures of phonological awareness, and in the second part, we present detailed descriptions and information about several currently available measures.

When Should Assessment of Phonological Awareness Be Conducted?

In most school programs, teachers should probably wait until the second semester of kindergarten to identify children who may require extra help in phonological awareness. When children enter school, their differences in phonological awareness are heavily influenced by their home language environment. Thus, children who score low on tests of phonological awareness early in the year may respond very well to systematic instruction in this area. Particularly when kindergarten children are exposed from the beginning of the year to activities designed to stimulate phonological awareness, by the beginning of the second semester, teachers will have a very good idea of which children are progressing slowly. The measures we discuss in this section can be used to support teacher judgments about the need for extra instruction.

When used in this way, the assessment of phonological awareness in kindergarten can be considered as part of an overall assessment effort to support the prevention of reading problems in young children. Assessment of phonological awareness in first- and second-grade children may also be warranted as a means to monitor the development of those who continue to experience difficulties in this area.

How Is Phonological Awareness Assessed?

Since researchers first began to study phonological awareness in the early 1970s, over 20 different tasks have been used to measure awareness of phonemes in words. These measures can be grouped into three broad categories: sound comparison, phoneme segmentation, and phoneme blending.

- *Sound comparison* tasks use a number of different formats that require children to make comparisons between the sounds in different words. For example, a child might be asked to indicate which word (of several) begins or ends with the same sound as a target word (e.g., "Which word begins with the same first sound as *cat: boy, cake,* or *fan?*"). Additionally, tasks that require children to generate words that have the same first or last sound as a target word fall in this category. Sound comparison tasks are particularly appropriate for kindergarten-age children, because these tasks do not require as fully explicit knowledge of phonemes as tasks that require children to pronounce or manipulate individual phonemes.

- *Phoneme segmentation* tasks require a relatively explicit level of phonemic awareness because they involve counting, pronouncing, deleting, adding, or reversing the individual phonemes in words. Common examples of this type of task require pronouncing the individual phonemes in words (e.g., "Say the sounds in *cat* one at a time"), deleting sounds from words (e.g., "Say *card* without saying the /d/ sound"), or counting sounds (e.g., "Put one marker on the line for each sound you hear in the word *fast*").

- *Phoneme blending* skill has been measured by only one kind of task. This is the sound blending task in which the tester pronounces a series of phonemes in isolation and asks the child to blend them together to form a word (i.e., "What word do these sounds make: /f/-/a/-/t/?"). Easier variants of the sound blending task for younger children can be produced by allowing the child to choose from two or three pictures the word that is represented by a series of phonemes.

An important point about these different kinds of tasks is that they all appear to be measuring essentially the same construct, or ability. Although some research (Yopp, 1988) has indicated that the tasks may vary in the complexity of their overall intellectual requirements, and there may be some differences between segmentation and blending tasks at certain ages (Wagner, Torgesen, & Rashotte, 1994), for the most part, they all seem to be measuring different levels of growth in the same general ability (Hoien, Lundberg, Stanovich, & Bjaalid, 1995; Stanovich, Cunningham, & Cramer, 1984). Sound comparison measures are easier and are sensitive to emergent levels of phonological awareness, whereas segmentation and blending measures are sensitive to differences among children during later stages of development involving refinements in explicit levels of awareness. Measures of sensitivity to rhyme (e.g., "Which word rhymes with *cat: leg* or *mat?*") are not included among measures of phonemic awareness because they appear to be measuring something a little different, and less predictive of reading disabilities, than those measures that ask children to attend to individual phonemes. For the same reason, measures of syllable awareness are not included in this group.

How Should You Select a Measure To Use in Your Assessment Program?

Although the most commonly used measures of phonological awareness appear to be measuring roughly the same construct, there are usually small differences in their predictive relationships with reading growth. In selecting the best measure to use in your classroom, at least three questions should be considered in addition to cost: (1) Is its degree of difficulty suitable for the children you will assess? (2) Does it have adequate measurement reliability? (3) What is the evidence for its ability to predict reading growth?

Degree of Difficulty

A given test may be a good indicator of relative strengths and weaknesses in phonological awareness among the children in your classroom and still not be an appropriate measure for your purposes. For example, if you are able to provide extra instruction only to the children who fall in the bottom 20% of your class, then you should use a test that is particularly sensitive to differences among children in the lower half of the class. This would probably be a relatively easy measure that does not discriminate well among the strongest children in your class, but that is very sensitive to differences among your weakest students. In contrast, if you used a more difficult measure, it might tell you who had the very strongest phonological skills in your class, but most of the children in the lower half of the class would obtain very low scores so that you could not differentiate among them easily.

If the children in your classroom generally come from backgrounds in which they have had rich preschool experiences with language and prereading activities, then a measure that has a slightly greater degree of difficulty may be most appropriate. In addition, if you are likely to be assessing children beyond kindergarten age, then you should select a measure that contains a sufficient number of more difficult items in order to provide sensitive measurement of individual differences beyond beginning levels of phonological awareness.

Measurement Reliability

Measurement reliability is simply the degree to which a test provides consistent assessment of a given construct. If a test does not have sufficient reliability, it cannot be counted on to serve as a useful supplement to teacher judgment by providing objective identification of children with different levels of phonological awareness. Test developers calculate reliability in a number of ways, and it is always expressed as a number between 0 and 1. Generally, tests with reliabilities above .85 are suitable for tracking the development of phonological awareness in individual children, and all of the measures discussed in this manual meet this criterion. A test's reliability should always be reported somewhere in the test manual.

Predictive Validity

Because the ultimate purpose for assessment of phonological awareness is to identify children who are likely to experience reading difficulties, it is important that the measure you select present evidence that it is strongly related to reading growth. Predictive relationships between measures of phonological awareness and reading are usually expressed as *correlation coefficients*.

A correlation coefficient is simply a number, derived from statistical calculations, that expresses the extent to which two variables are related to one another. For variables that are positively related to one another (i.e., when one is higher, the other also tends to be higher), such as phonological awareness and reading, correlation coefficients can range between 0 and 1, with predictive correlations for most measures of phonological awareness ranging between .6 and .8.

For practical purposes of identifying children who may be in need of extra support in the development of phonological awareness, small differences in the predictive strength of various measures are of little importance. However, other things being equal (e.g., cost, time and ease of administration), relative differences in predictive strength should be considered in selecting a measure of phonological awareness to use in the classroom or clinic.

Teachers and psychologists should also be alert to the fact that correlations between tests that are given *concurrently* (at the same time) are usually higher than those that are given predictively. Thus, when manuals report the relationship between a given measure of phonological awareness and reading, it is important to determine the length of time that elapsed between the measure of phonological awareness and the measure of reading. Ideally, measures should report the strength of the relationship between measures of phonological awareness administered in kindergarten and measures of reading administered in first or second grade.

Information Provided About Measures of Phonological Awareness

To make it easier for you to compare measures of phonological awareness, all the descriptions in this section are presented in a similar format. The format includes the following information:

- A description of the test
- Ages for which the test is applicable and issues in administration (e.g., the training required, whether it can be administered in groups)

- Example items
- Information on test reliability and validity
- Types of scores that are available
- Ordering information
- General comments about appropriateness for various purposes

In this section, we discuss eight tests that are presently available for teachers and other professionals to use in assessing phonological awareness. Some of these instruments have been through formal standardization procedures so that a given child can be compared to a random sample of other children of the same age or grade. These instruments, for example, can indicate what percentage of all children in the standardization sample (usually 100 to 200 children of the same age) obtained scores lower than the child who is being assessed. This kind of information is useful in estimating how extreme a given child's performance is compared to a large group of other children.

Being able to compare children's performance against that of a broadly based normative sample can also help to indicate what proportion of children in a class or school may be in need of special help to support their growth in phonological awareness. The proportion of children who come to school delayed in the development of phonological awareness will depend somewhat on specific aspects of their preschool language and literacy environment. Tests with national norms can help to pinpoint classes or schools in which a special effort must be made to enhance phonological awareness in children prior to or during reading instruction. For example, a classroom in which 75% of the children performed below the 20th percentile (in the bottom 20% of all children) will require more instructional resources to prepare children for learning to read than a classroom in which only 10% of the children scored that low.

A number of tests described in this section do not have normative information. Nevertheless, these tests can be useful as informal assessment instruments for monitoring the progress of children. If these instruments are used regularly, teachers will quickly become acquainted with their value in selecting the children who are most at risk for reading difficulties in their classroom. If classroom resources allow extra help for a fixed number of children (say, 20% to 30%), then these measures can be used immediately to identify the group of children within a classroom whose awareness of the phonological structure of words is least developed. Finally, these measures can be very useful in understanding which children are responding well to a given level or method of intervention, and which are not.

Tests Described in this Section

The tests discussed in this section differ from one another in at least two important ways. The most important distinction is between those tests that have been standardized on an appropriate national sample and those tests that have not been standardized. The second distinction is between tests that assess only phonological awareness and those that also provide measurement of other relevant skills, such as letter knowledge or rapid automatic naming. We first discuss three tests that have been standardized, and then present information about five nonstandardized tests. The tests we discuss are the following:

Standardized Tests

Comprehensive Test of Phonological Processes

The Phonological Awareness Test

Test of Phonological Awareness

Nonstandardized Tests

Lindamood Auditory Conceptualization Test

Rosner Test of Auditory Analysis

Test of Awareness of Language Segments

Test of Invented Spelling

Yopp–Singer Test of Phoneme Segmentation

Comprehensive Test of Phonological Processes

Description of Test

The *Comprehensive Test of Phonological Processes* (CTOPP) (Wagner, Torgesen, & Rashotte, 1999) provides assessment in three areas of phonological skill in individuals from age 5 through adulthood. The three types of phonological skill measured by the test are phonological awareness, rapid automatic naming, and verbal short-term memory. Tasks assessing all three of these areas are both predictive (Wagner et al., 1997) and diagnostic (Torgesen & Wagner, 1999) of reading disabilities, although phonological awareness and rapid automatic naming generally have the strongest relationships with the growth of word reading skills. The CTOPP was developed with support of a grant from the National Institute of Child Health and Human Development, and all of its subtests are patterned directly after tasks that have been widely used in previous research.

Appropriate Ages and Issues in Administration

The CTOPP is a diagnostic test designed for administration by individuals who have had adequate formal training in test administration and interpretation. It must be administered individually, and it takes about 20 minutes to administer the three core phonological awareness subtests to children ages 5 to 7, and about 15 minutes to administer the two core subtests to individuals ages 7 and older. Norms are provided for individuals ages 5-0 through 24-11, but adult norms should be applicable across a much broader age span because performance on these tests is very stable after about age 16.

Example Items

Although the CTOPP contains subtests that measure three different kinds of phonological processing skill, we focus only on the measures of phonological awareness. Altogether, the test contains six different measures of phonological awareness, although some of the subtests are used in the core battery and some are designated as supplemental subtests. The core measures for children ages 5 and 6 are Phoneme Elision, Blending Words, and Sound Matching, and the single supplemental test is Blending Nonwords. The core phonological awareness subtests for ages 7 through adulthood are Phoneme Elision and Blending Words, whereas Blending Nonwords, Segmenting Words, Segmenting Nonwords, and Phoneme Reversal are supplemental subtests at these age levels. Slightly different subtests are given at different ages to preserve maximum measurement sensitivity across the broad age span of the test. Example items from each of the core subtests follow.

▶ **Phoneme Elision**

Easy Item: "Say *popcorn*. Now say *popcorn* without saying *corn*." The item is correct if the child responds, "pop."

Harder Item: "Say *flame*. Now say *flame* without saying /f/." The item is correct if the child responds, "lame."

▶ **Blending Words**

Easy Item: "What word do these sounds make? s-un." The item is correct if the child responds, "sun."

Harder Item: "What word do these sounds make? /t/-/e/-/s/-/t/-/i/-/f/-/ie/." The item is correct if the child responds, "testify."

▶ **Sound Matching**

On this subtest, a picture book is used that has pictures of all the words that the examiner pronounces. The examiner points to each picture as it is named.

Easy Item: "Which word starts with the same sound as *pan: pig, hat,* or *cone?*" The correct answer is "pig."

Harder Item: "Which word ends with the same sound as *face: cake, fish,* or *mice?*" The correct answer is "mice."

Information on Test Reliability and Validity

Reliability

Estimates of test–retest and internal consistency reliability for the individual subtests and for composite scores made from combining the core subtests are provided in the manual. Reliabilities are reported at yearly intervals between ages 5 and 17, and for 18- to 24-year-olds combined. In Table 2.1, we report the average values across all ages. The average internal consistency reliabilities of all the subtests fall within the acceptable range, and the reliabilities of the composite scores indicate that they are adequate for individual diagnostic purposes.

Validity

Various kinds of evidence for the validity of measurement provided by the CTOPP are presented in the manual, but we focus on the predictive and concurrent relationships between performance on the phonological awareness tests and reading ability. When the core subtests from the CTOPP were administered to children at the beginning of kindergarten and first grade (Wagner et al., 1997), the relationship of the composite scores to reading a year later was .71 for the kindergarten tests and .80 for the first-grade tests. These values indicate that the composite scores from the CTOPP have very high predictive validity during the period when children are first learning to read.

Table 2.1

Average Reliabilities for the Phonological Awareness Subtests of the
Comprehensive Test of Phonological Processes Across Age Levels

Measure	Test–Retest	Internal Consistency
Subtest		
Phoneme Elision	.88	.89
Blending Words	.88	.84
Sound Matching	.83	.93
Blending Nonwords	.76	.81
Phoneme Reversal	.79	.89
Segmenting Words	.77	.89
Segmenting Nonwords	.81	.90
Composite Scores		
Ages 5–6	.79	.95
Ages 7–24	.78	.90

Note. Data from Tables 6.1 (p. 64) and 6.4 (pp. 74–75) of the Examiner's Manual of the *Comprehensive Test of Phonological Processing,* by R. K. Wagner, J. K. Torgesen, and C. A. Rashotte, 1999, Austin, TX: PRO-ED.

During development, the CTOPP was administered to 603 students in Grades K through 5. When the age level of students is controlled, the concurrent relationship of the core phonological awareness tests to word reading ability was as follows: Phoneme Elision, .73; Blending Words, .62; and Sound Matching, .58. The CTOPP was also administered to 73 students at a reading clinic who were in Grades K through 12, with a median age of 9. Again with age partialled out of the relationship, the correlation between Phoneme Elision and reading was .65; relationships for Blending Words and Sound Matching were .59 and .46, respectively.

Types of Scores Available

Both standard and percentile scores are available for each subtest, as well as composite scores in phonological awareness, rapid naming, and verbal memory. In addition, grade and age equivalent scores are available for each of the subtests and composites.

Ordering Information

The CTOPP may be ordered from PRO-ED, Inc., 8700 Shoal Creek Boulevard, Austin, TX 78757-6897; phone: 800/897-3202.

General Comments About Uses

The CTOPP is a soundly constructed test that is based on a thoroughly tested model of phonological processing and that uses tests of phonological awareness that have been well studied in research. Together with the measures of rapid automatic naming and verbal short-term memory included on the test, the CTOPP should prove to be a valuable aid in the diagnosis of phonologically based reading disabilities. The composite scores in phonemic awareness are also highly predictive of early reading growth, suggesting that they would be very useful in early identification of children who should be provided with more intensive reading instruction to prevent reading failure.

 # The Phonological Awareness Test

Description of Test

The Phonological Awareness Test (PAT) (Robertson & Salter, 1997) contains five measures of phonemic awareness, plus measures of word and syllable segmentation and a measure of sensitivity to rhyme. It also contains subtests that measure knowledge of letter–sound correspondences, phonemic decoding (ability to read phonetically regular nonwords), and invented spelling. It is actually a comprehensive test of phonological sensitivity and phonemic reading ability. All tests were normed on a national sample of children ranging from 5 to 10 years of age.

Appropriate Ages and Issues in Administration

The PAT can be given to children 5 years of age and older. Although norms extend only through age 9, the authors believe information useful for planning instruction may be obtained for children older than 10. The test should be given by someone who is professionally trained in analyzing the phonological structure of speech, such as a speech–language pathologist, learning disability teacher, reading specialist, or special education consultant. The test must be given individually, and it takes about 40 minutes to administer when all sub-tests are given. Administration time can be cut substantially by administering only a few of the subtests, although this will reduce somewhat the reliability of the testing.

Example Items

Although the PAT contains measures of sensitivity to rhyme, as well as ability to segment words and syllables, these subtests are not discussed here because, as discussed earlier in this manual, they appear to provide measures of slightly dif-ferent constructs from measures that assess awareness at the level of phonemes. Five measures of phonemic awareness are included on the PAT.

▶ **Segmentation of Phonemes**

> **Example Item:** "I'm going to say a word, and then I'll say each sound in the word. Listen carefully. *Cat* (pause) /k/-/a/-/t/. Now tell me the sounds in *off*."

The child receives credit if all sounds are given in the proper order. There are 10 items.

▶ **Isolation**

> **Example Item:** "I'm going to say a word, and I want you to tell me the beginning or first sound in the word. What's the beginning sound in the word *cat*?" The child should respond, "/k/."

There are 30 items, 10 each for the first, last, and middle sounds in short words.

▶ **Deletion**

> **Example Item:** "I'm going to ask you to say a word and then to say it again without one of its sounds. Say *cat*" (student responds). "Now say it again, but don't say /k/." The child should respond, "at."

There are 10 items.

▶ **Substitution**

> The first part of this subtest requires the use of colored blocks to show the different sounds in words.

Example Item: "I'm going to show you how to make the word *fun* with these blocks. Each block is one sound of the word." The examiner illustrates the relationship between blocks and sounds by touching each block while saying /f/-/u/-/n/. The examiner then says, "Now, watch while I change *fun* to *run*." This change is illustrated by replacing the first block with a different colored block. "Now it says *run*."

There are 10 test items that require children to show which sounds have changed on examples like *map* to *mop*, or *tip* to *tick*.

There are also 10 test items that do not involve blocks. "Say *cow*. Now change /k/ to /h/." The child should respond, "how."

▶ **Blending**

Example Item: "I'll say the sounds of a word. You guess what the word is. What word is this? /p/-/o/-/p/" (pronouncing the phonemes at one per second). The child must pronounce "pop" correctly to receive credit.

There are 10 items.

Information on Test Reliability and Validity

Reliability

Estimates of both test–retest and internal consistency reliability are provided in the PAT manual. The values reported here are those that apply to the section of each subtest that measures awareness at the phonemic level. In the manual, reliabilities are reported at half-year age intervals between 5 and 10 years of age. In Table 2.2, we report the average values across all ages.

Measurement reliability would undoubtedly be improved if more than a single subtest were used to estimate level of phonological awareness at any given age. However, because of the way the reliabilities are reported in the manual, it is not possible to estimate the overall measurement reliability of combinations of subtests assessing phonemic awareness.

Validity

Values for the predictive validity of the PAT are not reported in the manual. Concurrent validity was established by contrasting the performance of groups of randomly selected children from the normative sample with samples of children who were identified as at risk for reading problems or as having reading problems. The total score on the PAT successfully discriminated between these two groups at five age levels between 5 and 10. The five individual measures of

Table 2.2
Average Reliabilities for *The Phonological Awareness Test* Across
Grade Levels

Subtest	Test–Retest	Internal Consistency
Segmentation	.71	.81
Isolation	.72	.89
Deletion	.71	.73
Substitution	.77	.82
Blending	.76	.74

Note. Data from Tables 4.1 through 4.3 (p. 91) in the Examiner's Manual of *The Phonological Awareness Test*, by C. Robertson and W. Salter, 1997, East Moline, IL: LinguiSystems.

phonemic awareness also successfully discriminated between these groups in 23 of 25 comparisons. The only nonsignificant differences were for the Segmentation and Isolation subtests at the oldest age levels.

Types of Scores Available

Because the PAT has been normed on a large sample of children, both percentiles and standard scores can be derived at all ages between 5 and 10 years. One potentially useful feature is that these types of scores can be derived for each subtest as well as for the total test.

Ordering Information

The PAT can be ordered from LinguiSystems, 3100 4th Avenue, East Moline, IL 61244-0747; phone: 800/776-4332.

General Comments About Uses

The PAT is a well-constructed, comprehensive measure of phonological awareness and phonemic reading skills. Although the letter knowledge and reading subtests were not discussed in this manual, they may provide a useful addition to professionals who wish to assess both phonemic awareness and print knowledge at the same time. Both the predictive validity of the overall test and the specific utility of the word-, syllable-, and rhyme-level subtests will need to be demonstrated in further research with the instrument. However, there is little doubt that a combination of measures at the phonemic level from this instrument will provide a very useful assessment of individual differences in children's level of phonemic awareness.

Test of Phonological Awareness

Description of Test

The *Test of Phonological Awareness* (TOPA) (Torgesen & Bryant, 1994) contains two subtests that both involve sound comparison activities. It was designed to provide a simple and efficient way to identify young children who were lagging behind in their development of phonemic awareness. It was developed with support of a grant from the National Institute of Child Health and Human Development (Torgesen, Bryant, Wagner, & Pearson, 1992), and it is nationally normed. Items on the test were developed to be most sensitive to individual differences in phonemic awareness at lower levels of ability.

Appropriate Ages and Issues in Administration

The TOPA is appropriate for administration to children in kindergarten through second grade. It is designed to be administered by teachers or aides, but those administering the test must be able to speak clearly and pronounce individual phonemes correctly.

There are two versions of the test, one for children in kindergarten (Kindergarten version) and one for children in first and second grades (Early Elementary version). Both versions come in the same test kit. The TOPA can be given either in groups or individually and takes from 15 to 20 minutes to administer. The entire testing can be done in one session or spread across two sessions depending on the time available for testing and children's attentional capacities.

Example Items

The Kindergarten version consists of 20 items that involve comparison of the first sounds in words. The first set of 10 items requires children to indicate which of three pictures begins with the *same* first sound as a target word, and the second set of 10 items asks them to indicate which of four pictures begins with a *different* first sound than the others.

After going through some brief exercises to ensure that the children understand the meaning of *same* and *different*, as well as how to mark the items, they are shown three example items such as the ones in Figure 2.1. The following directions go with this type of item, referred to as Initial Sound–Same (see Figure 2.1): "Look at the first picture. The first picture is *bat*. Now look at the other three pictures: *horn, bed, cup*. Mark the one picture that begins with the same sound as *bat* (pause). You should have marked *bed* because *bat* and *bed* begin with the same sound, /b/."

The other type of item on the Kindergarten version of the TOPA is called Initial Sound–Different. An example of this type of item and the directions that go with it are as follows (see Figure 2.2): "Look at the pictures, *knife, fork, neck, nest*. Mark the one picture that has a different first sound than the other three (pause). You should have marked *fork*, because *knife, neck*, and *nest* begin with the same sound, /n/. *Fork* begins with a different sound, /f/."

Figure 2.1. Example of Initial Sound–Same item from the *Test of Phonological Awareness*. *Note.* From Student Booklet, Kindergarten Version, *Test of Phonological Awareness*, by J. K. Torgesen and B. Bryant, 1994, Austin, TX: PRO-ED. Copyright 1994 by PRO-ED, Inc. Reprinted with permission.

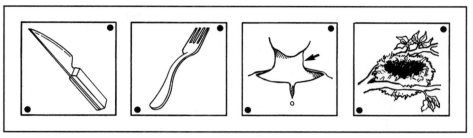

Figure 2.2. Example of Initial Sound–Different item from the *Test of Phonological Awareness*. *Note.* From Student Booklet, Kindergarten Version, *Test of Phonological Awareness*, by J. K. Torgesen and B. Bryant, 1994, Austin, TX: PRO-ED. Copyright 1994 by PRO-ED, Inc. Reprinted with permission.

The only difference between the Kindergarten and Early Elementary versions of the TOPA is that in the Early Elementary version, comparisons are made between the last sounds in words rather than in the first sounds. Attending to last sounds in words is more difficult than first sounds; thus, the items on the Early Elementary version are more difficult.

Information on Test Reliability and Validity

Reliability

The test manual provides two types of test reliability for the TOPA. Internal consistency reliabilities average .90 between kindergarten and second grade (ages 5 through 7). The test–retest reliability, with 6 weeks between testings, for the Kindergarten version was .94, whereas for children in the beginning of first grade, it was .77 over 8 weeks. The lower test–retest reliability for the first graders may reflect the impact of reading instruction, from which some children profit more than others.

Validity

The TOPA manual gives values for both concurrent validity and predictive validity. The reported correlation between the Early Elementary version of the TOPA and a measure of phonemic reading ability (the Word Attack Subtest from the *Woodcock Reading Mastery Tests–Revised*, Woodcock, 1987) in November of first grade was .66. When the Kindergarten version of the TOPA was given in April to a sample of children from an elementary school serving an area with a relatively low socioeconomic status and heavy minority population, the correlation with phonemic reading ability a year later was .62. Both of these values indicate that the TOPA is sufficiently predictive of early reading difficulties to warrant use as a means to identify children in need of special intervention to help prevent later reading problems.

Types of Scores Available

Because the TOPA was normed on a national sample of children, a variety of scores can be derived to show how an individual child compares to other children of the same age. These scores include percentiles and several types of standard scores.

Ordering Information

The TOPA may be ordered from PRO-ED, Inc., 8700 Shoal Creek Boulevard, Austin, TX 78757-6897; phone: 800/897-3202.

General Comments About Uses

The TOPA is an excellent test for use in identifying kindergarten children who are lagging behind their peers in the development of phonological awareness. It is particularly useful for classroom teachers because it can be administered to groups of children. It may also be used to identify children who are struggling with phonological awareness in first and second grades, but is not sensitive to differences among children in the upper half of the distribution because, even in the Early Elementary version, the items are too easy.

Lindamood Auditory Conceptualization Test

Description of Test

The *Lindamood Auditory Conceptualization Test* (LAC) (C. H. Lindamood & P. C. Lindamood, 1979) has been used for many years in clinical work with children with reading disabilities. The test provides "recommended minimum scores" for Grades K through 6, with a separate estimate for the range of Grade 7 through adult. These estimates are based on the authors' extensive clinical experience with the test, and they suggest that children who score below these levels will likely have difficulties acquiring phonetic decoding skills. The test requires children to indicate the number, identity, and order of phonemes in words using colored blocks.

Appropriate Ages and Issues in Administration

The LAC can be given to children as young as kindergarten age and can also be administered to adults. A more difficult version of the LAC is currently being developed which will provide finer discriminations of individual differences in phonological awareness in older children and adults. The test can be given by anyone who has been trained in its use. However, some parts of its administration are complex and require careful feedback to the person being tested, so sufficient time must be budgeted to learn proper administration procedures. The test must be given individually and, depending on the age of the child, takes between 15 and 25 minutes to administer.

Example Items

The LAC has two levels, Category I and Category II. Category I items are included primarily to determine whether the child can understand how to represent the number, order, and identity of sounds with colored blocks, and Category II actually assesses phonemic awareness.

The child begins with some preparatory items designed to help him or her understand the directions of the test. The child is requested to do such things as, "Show me three blocks that are the same color," or "Show me three blocks, and make only the first and the last one the same." On these items, the examiner is supposed to provide various types of instructive feedback.

Category I items begin with the instruction, "I want you to use these blocks to show me how many sounds I make, and whether they are the same or different." The examiner then says /z/-/z/, and demonstrates that the child should place two blocks of the same color. After several instructive items of this type, the child performs items varying in difficulty, from "Show me /p/-/p/-/p/" to "Show me /t/-/t/-/ch/."

Category II items require the child to represent the order, number, and identity of sounds in syllables with colored blocks. After thoroughly demonstrating what is required, the child starts with an item like, "Show me /i/." If the child correctly places one block, the next item is, "If that says /i/, show me /ip/." A series of 12 increasingly difficult items is chained together in this manner, until the final two items, which are "If that says /aps/, show me /asp/." And then, "If that says /asp/, show me /sasp/."

Information on Test Reliability and Validity

Reliability

The LAC manual presents strong evidence for the test's concurrent and predictive validity, but the information on test reliability is weakened by the use of inappropriate statistical analyses. The only reliability value reported is a test–retest correlation (.96) , and this number is spuriously inflated because it was derived from testing four children at each age level in Grades K through 12 on alternate forms of the test. Including children with such a wide age span in the reliability sample artificially inflates the reliability estimate because there is a large age-related difference in performance among the children.

Validity

The LAC manual provides extensive information on concurrent validity of the test, as well as an estimate of predictive validity. The LAC and the reading portion of the *Wide Range Achievement Test* (Jastak & Jastak, 1978), which is a measure of word reading ability, were given to groups of children in Grades K through 12. The average correlation between the LAC and the reading test was .73, with values for each age ranging from .66 to .81. In terms of predictive validity, the manual reports values ranging from .88 to .98 for relationships between the LAC administered in September of first grade and reading at the end of first grade as measured by several different tests.

Types of Scores Available

Because the LAC has not undergone formal norming procedures, percentile and standard scores are not available. However, the authors do provide values for "recommended minimum scores" at each grade level from K through 6, with a separate estimate for adults. These scores are provided to guide both preventive and remedial interventions. The authors supplement these recommended minimum scores with extensive case discussions to illustrate the meaning of scores in various ranges on the LAC.

Ordering Information

The LAC may be ordered from PRO-ED, Inc., 8700 Shoal Creek Boulevard, Austin, TX 78757-6897; phone: 800/897-3202.

General Comments About Uses

The LAC provides an excellent assessment of phonemic awareness in older children and adults. Its use as a screening instrument in kindergarten is limited by both the complexity of the test itself and the time and training required to administer it. It is recommended for use as part of a diagnostic battery to examine the reasons for reading failure in children in second grade and older.

Rosner Test of Auditory Analysis

Description of the Test

The *Rosner Test of Auditory Analysis* (Rosner, 1975) is the oldest published test of phonemic awareness, and it has been widely used in research. It is a relatively brief test, with 13 items involving the deletion of phonemes from words, and it is easy to give, score, and interpret.

Appropriate Ages and Issues in Administration

The test can be given to children from kindergarten through late elementary school, but will be most sensitive to individual differences in phonemic awareness among children in Grades K through 2. It can be administered by teachers or aides and takes about 5 to 10 minutes to complete. The only difficult part in administration is learning to pronounce individual phonemes properly.

Example Items

The test begins with items involving segmentation of compound words and syllables but rapidly shifts to items involving deletion of phonemes. Directions for the first practice item are, "Let's play a word game. Say *cowboy* (allow child to respond). Now say it again, but don't say *boy*." The child should respond, "cow."

Sample items involving phoneme deletion are, "Say *coat*. Now say it again, but don't say /k/," and "Say *stale*. Now say it again, but don't say /t/." The correct answers for these two items, respectively, are "oat" and "sale."

Information on Test Reliability and Validity

Reliability

Rosner does not present reliability information in his description of the test. However, tests used in research that include items similar to those on the Rosner test report acceptable levels of reliability (Wagner et al., 1994).

Validity

Rosner also does not present formal information about the predictive validity of this test, but numerous studies have found that these types of items not only are strongly predictive of reading failure in young children (Wagner et al., 1994) but also are very sensitive in differentiating older children who have reading disabilities from children who read normally (Fletcher et al., 1994).

Types of Scores Available

Because this test is not normed, only raw scores are available. Rosner does provide values for "expected" performance at various age levels, based on his experience giving the test to many children. For example, raw scores from 1 to 3 would be expected in kindergarten, 4 to 9 in first grade, and 10 to 13 in second grade.

Ordering Information

This test is available from the updated book in which it is published: *Helping Children Overcome Learning Disabilities* (3rd ed.), by J. Rosner, 1993, New York: Walker & Company, Publishers.

General Comments About Uses

This is an excellent test for a quick assessment of relative levels of phonological awareness within kindergarten, first-grade, and second-grade classrooms.

The only drawback is the absence of norms, but that should not prevent teachers from finding it useful in identifying children within their classrooms whose phonemic awareness is least well developed.

Test of Awareness of Language Segments

Description of the Test

The *Test of Awareness of Language Segments* (TALS) (Sawyer, 1987) measures children's ability to segment words in sentences, syllables in words, and sounds in words. The total score on the test represents a combination of scores on two or three of the subtests, depending on the age of the child to whom the test is administered. The test does not have norms, but the author provides separate cutoff scores for kindergarten-aged children and for children in first grade or older. The cutoff scores are based on extensive experience with the test in both research studies and clinical practice.

Appropriate Ages and Issues in Administration

The test can be given to anyone from age 4½ years through adulthood, although reliability and validity have been established only for children ages 4½ to 7 years. The test must be administered individually, and it takes about 15 to 20 minutes to administer, depending on the age of the child. Anyone familiar with the directions, and with the ability to accurately segment the sounds in words, can administer the test.

Example Items

The basic procedure of marking language segments with colored blocks is established in the first subtest (Part A), which involves segmenting sentences into words. Through demonstration and modeling, the child learns that each block is to stand for one word in the sentence. Children must perform satisfactorily on Part A by segmenting sentences into individual words before they are administered the other two parts of the test. Upon completion of Part A, children 4 years, 6 months to 5 years, 6 months take Part B, which involves dividing words into syllables, and representing individual syllables with colored blocks. Children who are older than 5 years, 7 months who successfully complete Part A are administered Part C, which involves segmenting single-syllable words into phonemes. If they do not perform satisfactorily on Part A, they take Part B. The words in Part C (segmenting words into sounds) are all single syllable, ranging from two to four phonemes in length. As with the other two tests, children are required to indicate the number of phonemes in words with colored blocks.

Information on Test Reliability and Validity

Reliability

Values for both internal consistency and test–retest reliability are reported in the manual for kindergarten and first-grade children. For kindergarten children, the average internal consistency value was .84, and for first graders it was .92. Test–retest reliability over a 1- to 2-week period was .89 for kindergarten children and .83 for first graders.

Validity

The predictive validity of the TALS was determined with samples of children ranging from 125 kindergartners to 247 first-graders. The correlation between the TALS administered in May of the kindergarten year with word reading ability measured at the end of first grade was .56. When the TALS was administered in October of first grade, its relationship with end-of-first-grade reading ability was .62. Both of these values suggest that the TALS can be used with reasonable confidence as part of a screening procedure to identify children who may be at risk for difficulties learning to read during first grade.

Types of Scores Available

Because the test is not normed, only raw scores are available. Based on her experience with the measure in both research and clinical practice, the test author has provided ranges of performance that are characteristic of kindergarten children falling in top, middle, and low groups of children. For children in first grade, she suggests performance levels that indicate children will have serious difficulty profiting from reading instruction in first grade.

Ordering Information

The TALS may be ordered from PRO-ED, Inc., 8700 Shoal Creek Boulevard, Austin, TX 78757-6897; phone: 800/897-3202.

General Comments About Uses

The manual for the TALS includes an entire chapter devoted to instructional implications for children who attain specific levels of performance on the test. The test has a solid basis in research and should prove useful as one element in a screening battery for kindergarten or first-grade children. The primary limitation of the test for use in large-scale screening activities is the time it takes to administer. Given that every child must be given at least two subtests, the efficiency of assessment may not be as great as with some other tests discussed in this manual.

 Test of Invented Spelling

Description of the Test

The *Test of Invented Spelling* (Mann, Tobin, & Wilson, 1987) measures more than simple phonemic awareness. Because it requires children to "represent as many of the sounds in words as they can" by spelling them, it also assesses knowledge of sound–letter correspondences. It is included here because it is very sensitive to individual differences in phonemic awareness and may actually be more predictive of later reading growth than many purely oral measures of phonemic awareness (Mann, 1993).

Appropriate Ages and Issues in Administration

The test is designed for children during the second semester of kindergarten, or as soon as they have acquired some rudimentary knowledge of letter–sound correspondences. This kind of test may not be appropriate once children begin formal instruction in spelling, as many of the words would simply be spelled correctly because they had been memorized. The test can be administered by teachers or aides to groups of children in less than 10 minutes. The scoring of the test is relatively complicated and requires a good understanding of phonetic relationships in spelling.

Example Items

Directions can be adapted to the circumstances of test administration but would go something like this: "I want you to try to try to write some words for me. I will say a word and you should write it as best you can. If you cannot write the whole word, write any of the sounds that you hear and any of the letters that you think might belong in that word." The first word on the test is *red*, followed by *name*, *bed*, and *lady*. There are 14 words on the test.

Information on Test Reliability and Validity

Reliability

Mann does not report reliability figures for this test, but the strength of its relationship to later reading development suggests that it is probably at least as reliable as most of the phonological awareness measures used with kindergarten children.

Validity

The predictive validity of the *Test of Invented Spelling* was assessed in a study (Mann, 1993) in which the spelling test was given in the second semester of kindergarten, and reading was assessed a year later. The correlation between the measure of invented spelling and phonetic reading ability was .61, while that with general word reading ability was .68. Both of these relationships are sufficiently strong to warrant the use of this measure to identify children who are at risk for reading difficulties.

Types of Scores Available

Because the test is not normed, only raw scores are available. Based on her experience with the measure, Mann (1993) suggests that scores below 5 at the end of kindergarten indicate a pronounced risk for reading problems in first grade.

Ordering Information

The test of invented spelling was first described in the following journal article: "Measuring Phonological Awareness Through the Invented Spellings of Kindergarten Children," by V. A. Mann, P. Tobin, and R. Wilson, 1987, *Merrill-Palmer Quarterly, 33*, 365–389. It is available from that source. This article has all the items for the test and the scoring instructions. To obtain a complete understanding of the test and its appropriate uses, we recommend reading the original article that reports its development.

General Comments About Uses

One useful feature about this test is that it can be given quickly to groups of children. In kindergarten classes where children are expected to know some of their letter sounds, it provides a very good way to assess both phonological awareness and beginning knowledge about print. At the beginning of first grade, for example, this test might be useful for identifying children who are most at risk for reading difficulties during the year. The test will not be sensitive to individual differences in phonological awareness in groups of children who have very limited knowledge of letters and their sounds.

Yopp–Singer Test of Phoneme Segmentation

Description of Test

The *Yopp–Singer Test of Phoneme Segmentation* (Yopp, 1995) is a brief test of children's ability to isolate and pronounce the individual phonemes in words. This type of task has been widely used in research on phoneme awareness over the last 20 years, and it is highly correlated with other measures of phoneme awareness (Yopp, 1988). The test is easy to give, score, and interpret.

Appropriate Ages and Issues in Administration

This test was designed for kindergarten children, but should also be appropriate for identifying children who are weak in phonological awareness during first grade. It can be administered by teachers or aides and must be given individually. It takes 5 to 10 minutes per child. It does not have norms.

Example Items

The test consists of 22 items that are all of the same type. Beginning the test, the child receives the following instructions:

> Today we're going to play a word game. I'm going to say a word and I want you to break the word apart. You are going to tell me each sound in the word in order. For example, if I say "old," you should say "/o/-/l/-/d/." (The administrator says the sounds, not the letters.) Let's try a few words together.

The practice items are *ride, go,* and *man.* All the items involve familiar words of only two or three phonemes.

Information on Test Reliability and Validity

Reliability

The article in which the test is described reports an internal consistency reliability of .95.

Validity

The Yopp–Singer test has impressive validity data derived from a 7-year longitudinal study in which the same children who were administered the phoneme segmentation test in kindergarten were followed through sixth grade. The segmentation test was administered in the second semester of kindergarten, and Table 2.3 gives the correlations between the test and various reading measures. All of the reading measures came from the *Comprehensive Test of Basic Skills* (1974). The Word Attack subtest measures phonetic reading skills and recognition of sight words; the Vocabulary subtest measures children's ability to identify a word associated with an orally presented category or definition; and

Table 2.3
Relationship of *Yopp–Singer Test of Phoneme Segmentation* to Later
Reading Scores

	Subtest			
Grade Level	Word Attack	Vocabulary	Comprehension	Total
1	.46	.66	.38	.62
2	.62	.72	.55	.67
3	.56	.66	.62	.67
4		.51	.62	.58
5		.56	.57	.59
6		.78	.66	.74

Note. Data from Table 2 in "A Test for Assessing Phonemic Awareness in Children," by H. K. Yopp, 1995, *The Reading Teacher*, 49, p. 25.

the Reading Comprehension subtest measures children's reading comprehension for both sentences and stories. The Total Score is the combined score on all the measures. The thing that is most impressive about these results is the continuing strong predictive relationship with reading growth through the end of sixth grade. A correlation of .74 with total reading score means that performance on the Yopp–Singer test in the second semester of kindergarten is highly correlated with overall reading ability 6 years later.

Types of Scores Available

This test has not been normed; only raw scores can be obtained.

Ordering Information

The Yopp–Singer test may be obtained free by copying it from the journal article in which it is described: "A Test for Assessing Phonemic Awareness in Young Children," by H. K. Yopp, 1995, *The Reading Teacher*, 49, pp. 20–29. The author provides a form in this article that is meant to be copied by teachers for use in their classrooms.

General Comments About Uses

The major difficulty with the Yopp–Singer test is that it may be too difficult to make fine discriminations among children in the lower ranges of phonemic awareness. The requirement to completely segment the word *dog* (first item on the test) may be too difficult for many populations of children in the United States. Although Yopp reports mean performance on the test of about 11 items correct in the second semester of kindergarten (children with average age of 70 months), her sample, as a whole, may have been stronger in phonemic awareness than many groups around the United States. For teachers who work with groups of children with traditionally high rates of reading problems, this test may be too difficult in kindergarten to discriminate among children in the lower ranges of ability.

Other than the issue of difficulty level for some groups of kindergarten children, this is a fine, reliable test of phonemic awareness. It could serve very usefully, for example, to monitor the growth of phonemic awareness in first-grade children as they learn to read.

INSTRUCTION IN PHONOLOGICAL AWARENESS

In this section, we describe eight instructional programs that have a primary focus on building phonological awareness in young children. Some of these programs are intended for use in the *regular classroom* setting, whereas others are designed for *small group or individual* instruction with children who require more intensive or explicit instruction in phonological awareness. In addition, we evaluate several computer programs that have been designed for use in stimulating phonemic awareness in young children. Before we present information about specific programs, however, we want to review both the goals of instruction in phonological awareness and some general teaching issues in this area.

Goals of Instruction in Phonological Awareness

Instruction in phonological awareness has two primary goals: (1) to help children learn to notice the phonemes in words, to discover their existence and distinctness, and (2) to help children make the "connection" between the phonemes in words and the letters of the alphabet. Good instruction in phonological awareness should *help children all the way to the discovery of the alphabetic principle*. Thus, although all phonological awareness training programs begin with oral language activities designed to help children attend to the individual sounds in words, they all should end, or overlap, with very simple phonics activities designed to show children how the sounds in words are represented by letters.

When children learn to speak their native language, most of their focus is on acquiring the meaning of words. They are occasionally corrected in their pronunciations, but the primary object of language learning is to understand the meaning of words in conversation. Because of the human capacity for language, the brain processes the phonemes in spoken words automatically and the child does not have to be consciously aware of them as individual sounds to understand speech. However, if a child is to understand the way that words are represented by print, he or she must become aware that words comprise individual sounds called phonemes. Thus, the first goal of instruction in phonological awareness is to provide discussion and activities that help to focus children's attention on the individual sounds in words. Good instruction in phonological awareness will help children learn to notice the *identity*, *number*, and *order* of sounds in words.

Although many children will automatically make the connection between the phonemes in oral language and the letters in print, many others will be helped significantly if this connection is made explicit for them through direct instruction. Several programs that provide instruction in phonemic awareness provide *simultaneous* instruction in sound–letter associations so that, once children can segment the sounds in words orally, they can begin to represent those segmented sounds with letters. Other programs provide more extensive instruction in phonemic awareness before introducing sound–letter associations, but they conclude with activities in which children use letters to represent the sounds they had previously been working with only in oral language activities. For example, toward the end of one instructional program (Torgesen & Bryant, 1993), children are taught a set of consonants and vowels that can be used to create a large number of three-letter words. The children then engage in a variety of discovery and practice activities that allow them to acquire beginning skills in "sounding out" simple printed words, and in spelling similar words by first segmenting the sounds and then using letters to represent the sounds. The important thing to remember is that the effectiveness of *all* instruction in phonological awareness will be improved if the connection between the phonemes in oral language and the letters in print is made explicitly and directly.

General Issues in Teaching Phonological Awareness

In this section, we list some of the most important general points about instruction in phonological awareness. Many of the instructional programs we describe later contain similar discussions, but we thought it would be useful to extract the most general issues that apply to all programs, and present them here. .

▶ 1. **Instruction in phonological awareness should begin with easier tasks and move toward more difficult tasks.**

This issue is so obvious, it almost goes without saying. However, it is important to note that explicit instruction in phonological awareness is developmentally appropriate for children as young as 4 or 5 years of age only if the concept is taught in a carefully structured way. Although we do not yet know precisely all of the potentially important steps in this instruction, we have a broad outline of the most important steps. For example, many programs begin with general listening activities designed to help children attend to sequences of individual sounds, and then move to activities that help children become aware of individual words in sentences, and then syllables in words. Other programs begin with activities involving rhyme in order to help children begin to focus on the sounds in words in addition to the words' meanings.

Instructional programs can follow a variety of paths after these initial, introductory activities, but it may be easiest for children to move next to activities that involve comparing words on the basis of first, last, and middle sounds. Sound comparison tasks do not require as fully explicit an awareness of sounds as is required by tasks that involve segmenting and pronouncing individual phonemes. Once children have some beginning proficiency with sound comparison tasks, they can be moved to training activities that involve segmenting beginning sounds and blending of onset–rhyme patterns (i.e., c-at, d-og). The final series of tasks should be those that involve completely segmenting the sounds in simple words, or blending all the sounds, or manipulating the sounds in words (e.g., "What word do we have if we say cat, but don't say the /k/ sound?").

▶ 2. **Instruction in phonological awareness should be a *regular* part of the curriculum.**

In the case of whole class instruction, activities to build phonological awareness should take place for 15 to 20 minutes every day throughout the entire kindergarten year. The daily focus on these activities will produce much more consistent growth than sporadic involvement or casual instruction that occurs at irregular intervals. For children who require more intensive instruction, small group or individual tutoring should be provided daily. One intensive program, for example, involves small group instruction delivered every day in 1/2-hour sessions for about 12 weeks.

▶ 3. **Teachers should expect that children will respond at widely varying rates to instruction in phonological awareness.**

Depending on their basic "talent" for processing phonological information, or on their previous experience with rhyming and letter activities, children will show very different rates of progress in the growth of their phonological awareness. Not only should classroom instructional activities be planned to accommodate wide differences in phonological ability among children, but also provision should be made to identify children who will require more intense or explicit instruction. By the beginning of the second semester of kindergarten, it should be very clear to teachers which children will require more intensive instruction, and these children should be taught in small groups or individually.

▶ 4. **Instruction in phonological awareness should involve both *analytic* and *synthetic* activities.**

Analytic activities require children to identify individual sounds within whole words (e.g., "Tell me some words that begin with the same sound as *dog*." "What is the first sound in *man*?" "If you say *man* without saying the /m/ sound, what word do you get?"). In contrast, synthetic activities involve blending together separately presented phonemes (e.g., "What word do these sounds make: /f/-/a/-/t/?"). Both of these kinds of skills with phonemes are important in learning to read and spell.

▶ 5. **Because the first goal of instruction in phonological awareness is to help children notice the individual sounds in words, teachers should speak slowly and carefully, and should pronounce individual sounds correctly.**

This is not as easy as it sounds. Often, the ability of teachers who have become good readers and spellers to "hear" individual sounds in words is distorted by their knowledge of a word's spelling. For example, they may feel that they hear four sounds in the word *church* because of the extra consonant after the vowel, but in fact, the letters (u) and (r) are blended into a single sound in this word. It would be a mistake to expect children to blend together the sounds /ch/-/u/-/r/-/ch to obtain the word *church*. Similarly, teachers may think there are four sounds in the word *pitch* because of the presence of the letter (t), whereas the word *pitch* rhymes with *rich*.

▶ 6. **It is not easy to pronounce individual phonemes correctly without some careful practice.**

Even with practice, it is impossible to pronounce phonemes individually without some distortion, because in speech they are always coarticulated with other phonemes. By coarticulation, we mean that the pronunciation of individual phonemes in words is always influenced to some degree by the phonemes that precede and follow them. For example, the mouth is shaped quite differently for the pronunciation of the phoneme /b/ when it occurs at the beginning of the words *beet* and *bought*. As mentioned earlier, speech is fluent because speakers overlap the pronunciation of individual phonemes when pronouncing words. However, this also makes it somewhat challenging to pronounce individual phonemes by themselves, because speakers are highly practiced in coarticulating them with surrounding phonemes.

To help children learn about the identity of individual phonemes, the teacher needs to keep the distortion in pronunciation of individual phonemes to a minimum. Some phonemes are harder to pronounce in isolation than others. In Table 3.1 we have listed the consonant phonemes together in three groups according to the difficulty they present in individual pronunciation. We have also given a few suggestions that may help teachers pronounce these phonemes properly during instruction.

▶ 7. **Methods to stimulate phonemic awareness in students are limited only by the creativity of teachers.**

Once teachers understand the general instructional goals of instruction in phonemic awareness, they should be able to expand broadly on the methods that are contained in the formal instructional programs discussed in this manual. Recent research on effective teaching of reading in first grade (Wharton-McDonald, Pressley, & Hampston, 1998) has shown that good teachers embed phonemic awareness instruction within many different types of activities throughout the day. Spelling and writing activities present many powerful opportunities for building phonemic awareness, and when teachers help children "think" about the decoding process during reading, they also have many opportunities to draw upon and expand children's developing phonemic awareness. For example, when teachers ask children to "think of a word that has those sounds in it and makes sense in this sentence," they are actually showing children how to use their phonemic awareness (generating lists of words that have similar sounds in them) in the service of identifying words in print.

▶ 8. **Instruction in phonological awareness should be fun for teachers and students.**

When children learn about the sounds in words, they are making "discoveries" about their language. One has only to observe the delight that children take in rhyming stories and rhyming games to know that playing with the sounds in words can be fun. Most of the training programs discussed in this manual embed activities to enhance phonological awareness in gamelike contexts. If kindergarten phonological awareness instruction is not fun, it is not being done properly.

Table 3.1
Pronunciation Suggestions for Individual Phonemes

Easy To Pronounce

/m/ (man)	/sh/ (division)
/n/ (nose)	/s/ (safe)
/f/ (face)	/z/ (zebra)
/v/ (vase)	/th/ (think)
/sh/ (shop)	/th/ (the)

Pronunciation Notes

These phonemes can all be "stretched out" without distorting them very much. The main thing to remember for phonemes such as /f/, /sh/, /s/, and /th/ is that the vocal cords are not used when making the sounds, so you need to put enough "air" into the pronunciation to be easily heard. Sometimes teachers add a vowel sound to these phonemes when they pronounce them, as in "nuh" for /n/ or "fuh" for /f/. It is not necessary to add vowel sounds to this group of consonants and, in fact, doing so will confuse children. Phonemes in this group should be pronounced by simply stretching out the sound, as in /ffffff/ or /nnnnnnn/.

Slightly Harder To Pronounce

/t/ (talk)	/ch/ (cheek)
/p/ (pink)	/w/ (water)
/k/ (kite)	/wh/ (what)
/ng/ (ring)	/h/ (help)
/l/ (lap)	

(continues)

Table 3.1 *Continued*

Pronunciation Notes

1. Some of these phonemes, such as /t/, /p/, /k/, and /ch/ are hard to isolate because they need to be pronounced strongly as "whispers." The vocal cords are not vibrating while you pronounce these sounds, so *no vowel sound* should follow the consonant sound (e.g., "tuh," "puh," "kuh").

2. Teachers also have a tendency to pronounce /l/ as "luh," but this will make it hard for children to blend the sound with other phonemes during sound blending activities. You do not need to follow the /l/ sound with a vowel; simply bring your tongue to the top of your mouth (behind the front teeth) and leave it there as you say the sound, /llllllll/.

3. The /ng/ sound is hard to learn to say by itself. The best way to practice saying it is to say a word such as "ring," and then notice what your mouth is doing at the end of the word. When you say the sound /ng/, put your mouth in the same position, and use your vocal chords.

4. The sound /h/ is difficult because you need to get enough energy in your "whisper" (do not follow it with a vowel by saying "huh") to be heard. You should be blowing a lot of air out when you say /h/, but should not be using your vocal chords.

5. Finally, the sounds /w/ and /wh/ are often confused with one another, particularly in Southern dialects. Thus, some speakers pronounce words like *what* and *win* as though they begin with the same first sound. Actually, the sound /wh/ should be pronounced with no vocalization (with just air coming out), whereas the /w/ sound should be vocalized from the beginning. In reality, this distinction is important primarily for spelling (if the words *when* and *win* are pronounced properly, it is obvious from listening to them that one begins with (*wh*) and the other (*w*). However, to avoid confusion when letter sounds and spelling are introduced, it may be best to avoid words with the /wh/ phoneme during instruction in phonological awareness.

Hardest to Pronounce

/d/ (dog)	/r/ (run)
/b/ (big)	/j/ (jump)
/g/ (gone)	

Pronunciation Notes

1. The primary difficulty with the phonemes /d/, /b/, /g/, and /j/ is that you need to vocalize (make your vocal cords vibrate) while you say them, which causes the tendency to lengthen the resulting vowel sound too much. Thus, people tend to say "duuuh" for /d/, and "buuh" for /b/. The art of good pronunciation with these phonemes is to make that vowel sound as short as possible.

(continues)

Table 3.1 *Continued*

Pronunciation Notes *(continued)*

2. The phoneme /r/ is probably the hardest one to pronounce in isolation. Typically, teachers pronounce it in one of two ways. It can be pronounced with a vowel sound at the beginning, as in "errrr," or the vowel sound can follow, as in "ruh." The pronunciation that is usually most helpful is similar to "ruh," as long as the vowel part is very short. For example, if you are asking a child to blend the sounds in *run*, it would be a mistake to say /err/-/u/-/n/, because then the child would be led to say "errun." Words in which the vowel sound comes before the /r/ are usually words such as *hurt, dart, her,* or *corn,* that contain what is called an r-controlled vowel. When blending these words, the teacher would say, for example, /k/-/or/-/n/ for corn.

Short Vowels

/a/ (apple)   /o/ (octopus)

/e/ (Eskimo)   /u/ (umbrella)

/I/ (Indian)

Pronunciation Notes

1. The major difficulty presented by vowel sounds is that their pronunciation varies with dialect. They are pronounced somewhat differently in various regions of the country, and there may be a mismatch between the way the teacher pronounces them and the way children in the class pronounce them. As long as the teacher allows reasonable latitude, this does not present as much of a problem in phonological awareness training as it does when children begin to learn the sounds associated with various letters.

2. At some point, it may be helpful to teach children that pronunciations for words "in books" may differ from the way they hear them pronounced in their home and neighborhood. It is important to learn about "book" sounds because this will be very helpful in spelling. Children who come to school speaking a very different dialect from the one in which instruction is offered frequently experience difficulties learning to read. One reason for this is that they have difficulty relating the sounds in their oral language to the way words are represented in print. Because it is critical for all children to acquire phonemic reading skills early in development, teachers must work especially hard with these children to ensure that they make the connection between the sounds in words and spellings in print.

Programs To Help Children Acquire Phonemic Awareness

In the remainder of this manual, we describe several kinds of curriculum materials that teachers can use to stimulate phonological awareness in individuals ranging in age from kindergarten to adulthood. Most of the materials are designed for young children, as this is the most appropriate time to offer this type of instruction. However, for individuals who continue to struggle in this area, perhaps because of a severe deficiency of "phonological talent," intensive programs have been designed to help them acquire phonemic awareness. The programs we discuss fall roughly into two categories: those designed for regular classroom instruction in either whole class or small group settings, and those designed for more intensive and explicit instruction for children who do not learn enough from programs offered in the regular classroom.

Programs for Regular Classroom Instruction

Ladders to Literacy

Phonemic Awareness in Young Children: A Classroom Curriculum

The Sounds Abound Program: Teaching Phonological Awareness in the Classroom

Sounds Abound Instructional Materials and Game

Programs for Small Group or Individualized Training

Launch into Reading Success Through Phonological Awareness Training

The Lindamood Phoneme Sequencing Program for Reading, Spelling, and Speech

Phonological Awareness Training for Reading

Road to the Code: A Phonological Awareness Program for Young Children

Computer Programs for Stimulating Phonemic Awareness

DaisyQuest and *Daisy's Castle*

Earobics

Read, Write, and Type

Waterford Early Reading Program—Level 1

Ladders to Literacy

Description of Program

The *Ladders to Literacy* curriculum comprises a Preschool Activity Book (Notari-Syverson, O'Connor, & Vadasy, 1998) and a Kindergarten Activity Book (O'Connor, Notari-Syverson, & Vadasy, 1998). Both books offer a range of activities to support instruction in each of the critical areas of emergent literacy: print and book awareness, phonological awareness, and oral language skills. As Joseph Jenkins suggested in the foreword to the Kindergarten Activity Book, "*Ladders to Literacy* provides teachers the comprehensive and developmentally appropriate emergent literacy curriculum they seek." The development of the activities in both books was supported by a lengthy (3- to 5-year) period of both basic and field research designed to evaluate the practicality and effectiveness of the activities when applied in appropriate educational settings.

Materials Included with Purchase

The materials for both the preschool and the kindergarten versions come in spiral-bound notebooks. Each book has an excellent discussion of the concept of emergent literacy, and of each of the three elements that contribute to it: print and book awareness, phonological awareness, and oral language skills. The books do not include materials to use in the activities, but provide a full description of the materials required, and most would be relatively easy for teachers to find or create from materials in their classrooms. Examples of some of the materials used in the kindergarten phonological awareness activities include pictures of rhyming words, a box of small toys, drawing materials, and pictures of words beginning with different first sounds. Both books also contain a description of interesting activities that parents can do with their children at home to support emergent literacy goals, and the Preschool Activity Book contains a checklist of emergent literacy skills that will allow teachers to establish the instructional needs of different children in their classes.

Range of Instructional Activities

Some activities in each book were designed to stimulate the development of phonological awareness. Neither book contains a tightly organized curriculum as is found in some of the other programs outlined in this manual, but the instructional activities are roughly ordered in a developmental sequence. Many of the activities can be used on multiple days and with different materials to build more generalized phonemic awareness skills. An important feature of both activity books is their careful attention to methods for teaching children who learn at different rates. Accompanying each activity are suggestions for teacher–child interactions that are classified as High Demand/Low Support, Medium Demand/Medium Support, or Low Demand/High Support. These instructional suggestions allow the program to be used with heterogeneous groups of children and provide the teacher with guidance about how to provide "scaffolded" support for children according to their needs.

Preschool Activity Book

The Preschool Activity Book contains a total of 19 activities that can be used to support development in the following:

- *Perception and Memory for Sounds and Words*—These activities are designed to help children listen to, remember, and interpret sounds in their environment.

- *Word Awareness*—These activities help children learn to identify individual words in sentences.

- *Rhyming*—Experience with nursery rhymes and rhyming activities helps children begin to pay attention to the sounds within words.

- *Alliteration*—Children learn to compare words, or generate lists of words, on the basis of common first sounds. This helps them begin to notice individual phonemes in words.

- *Blending*—Children are taught first to blend words divided into onsets and rimes, and then to blend individual phonemes to produce words.

- *Segmentation*—Children gain initial experience in pronouncing the individual syllables and sounds in words.

Kindergarten Activity Book

The Kindergarten Activity Book also contains 19 activities to be used in stimulating the development of phonemic awareness. The activities in this book cover essentially the same range of skills as in the preschool book, but there is more emphasis on integrating print knowledge with phonemic awareness. For example, in "First Sound Bingo" children must identify the first sounds in words and then match them to an appropriate letter, and in "Segmenting into Three Phonemes," after children can successfully segment words as they touch a box to represent each sound, they can be encouraged to place letters in the boxes to represent the sounds.

Research Base To Support Its Use

The *Ladders to Literacy* curriculum is supported by a very strong research base. Many of the procedures included in the activities have been carefully evaluated in focused research (i.e., O'Connor, Jenkins, & Slocum, 1995; Slocum, O'Connor, & Jenkins, 1993). Furthermore, complete sets of the activities have been evaluated in classroom settings that were similar to the conditions under which the program is likely to be applied (O'Connor, Notari-Syverson, & Vadasy, 1996). This research found that children who did the *Ladders to Literacy* activities in kindergarten made greater improvement in reading and writing skills than children exposed to a more standard kindergarten curriculum. A study that tested the literacy skills of these children 1 year later (O'Connor et al., 1998) found significant remaining effects on literacy development of children who had participated in the *Ladders to Literacy* curriculum.

Ordering Information

The *Ladders to Literacy* activity books can be obtained from Brookes Publishing Company, P.O. Box 10624, Baltimore, MD 21285-0624; phone: 800/638-3775.

General Comments About Use

The *Ladders to Literacy* materials provide the essential, or core, activities for a complete emergent literacy curriculum in preschool and kindergarten. Although the range of phonemic awareness activities is not as large as in some of the other programs described in this manual, both activity books contain an extensive set of activities to also stimulate print and book awareness, and oral language development. Another strong feature of these materials is their careful attention to methods for adapting instruction to children with different instructional needs. This attention to "scaffolding" during instruction will allow the program to be used with relatively heterogeneous groups of children in whole class interventions, and with small groups of children who may need more intensive, or focused instruction.

Phonemic Awareness in Young Children: A Classroom Curriculum

Description of the Program

Phonemic Awareness in Young Children: A Classroom Curriculum (Adams, Foorman, Lundberg, & Beeler, 1997) is a complete, organized curriculum in phonological awareness that is appropriate for kindergarten classrooms, as well as first graders who are lagging behind their peers in the development of phonological awareness. It was translated from a program developed by Ingvar Lundberg and used in one of the early and most successful studies of phonological awareness training in the research literature (Lundberg, Frost, & Peterson, 1988). It is essentially a carefully sequenced series of gamelike activities that can be used with large or small groups to build phonological awareness in young children. In a typical kindergarten classroom, the program contains enough activities to occupy 15 to 20 minutes a day for 8 months of the school year. It contains an excellent discussion of the concept of phonological awareness and its relation to reading growth, and offers many helpful suggestions for teaching techniques in this area.

Materials Included with Purchase

This program is contained in a single teacher's manual, which describes all 51 activities and how to sequence them in instruction. It also contains many lists of words that can be used in the activities. Some of the activities require that the teacher supply materials such as pictures, a ball of yarn, or colored paper. None of the materials would be difficult for a typical kindergarten teacher to locate or develop. The manual also includes a number of group-administered phonological awareness tests that can be used to monitor children's progress. Finally, an extensive selection of support materials is listed that includes a list of rhyming and alliteration books that can be used by parents and teachers to get children thinking about the sounds in words.

Range of Instructional Activities

This program contains a series of activities that are graded in difficulty, along with a recommended sequence for introducing the activities. The goal of all the activities is for the children to have fun while learning to listen for the sounds in words. Following is the recommended sequence of activities in the program.

Listening Games—These introductory activities are designed to sharpen children's ability to listen selectively to sounds in their environment.

Rhyming Activities—These activities involve listening to rhyming sentences and stories, generation of rhymes, and judgments about rhyming words to introduce the idea of listening for the sounds in words.

Sentences and Words—These activities are included to help children begin to learn about listening for the parts within wholes. They acquire an awareness that sentences are made of words.

Syllables—Children learn more about listening for the parts within wholes, and also about putting parts together to make wholes while they become aware of syllables in words. These activities teach children to count syllables in words and blend syllables together to make words.

Initial and Final Sounds—These are the first activities that introduce children to the individual sounds in words. Depending on the pace of the class, this stage of instruction might be reached by late October or November. The children begin with a series of activities with first sounds, such as comparing first sounds in words, pronouncing the first sounds, or changing the first sounds to make other words, and then do similar activities with last sounds.

Phonemes—These activities typically take place during the second semester of kindergarten, and involve full analysis and pronunciation of individual sounds in words as well as activities to teach children to blend sounds together to make words. A variety of concrete materials, such as blocks, chips, or pieces of paper, are used to represent individual sounds in words.

Letters—These activities come toward the end of the year. Children are taught the letters used to represent a small number of consonant and vowel sounds, and then practice using these letters to represent the sounds in words in both reading and spelling activities.

Research Base To Support Its Use

This program was first evaluated in a study reported by Lundberg et al. (1988) that was conducted in Denmark. The study showed not only that the children improved significantly in phonological awareness, but also that the children who received the program became better readers and spellers than those who did not. The English translation of the program was evaluated in a study reported by Foorman, Francis, Shaywitz, Shaywitz, and Fletcher (1996). Using the program with inner-city children in the Houston Public Schools produced significant enhancement of their growth in phonological awareness by the end of the kindergarten year.

Ordering Information

The program may be obtained from Brookes Publishing Company, P.O. Box 10624, Baltimore, MD 21285-0624; phone: 800/638-3775.

General Comments About Use

This excellent program is strongly recommended for use in kindergarten classrooms. It is also recommended for use with weaker students during first grade. It is teacher friendly in design and well organized. The activities should be fun for both teachers and children, and there are clear directions on how to deliver the instruction. The only obvious limitation of the program at present is that it does not supply all the materials required to deliver the instruction. However, the extra materials that are required should be readily available in any kindergarten or first-grade classroom.

The Sounds Abound Program: Teaching Phonological Awareness in the Classroom

Description of the Program

The Sounds Abound Program (Lenchner & Podhajski, 1997) (formerly known as *Sound Start*) contains activities to stimulate phonological awareness that are appropriate for preschool through first-grade children. It was developed out of experience at the Stern Center for Language and Learning in Williston, Vermont, and grew out of the efforts of Orna Lenchner and others to help classroom teachers build phonological awareness in their students. It is designed to serve as a regular classroom curriculum in phonological awareness primarily for the kindergarten year, and contains activities to teach rhyme, syllable, and phoneme awareness. Two activities at the end of the program help children practice using letters to represent the first sound in words.

Materials Included with Purchase

The Sounds Abound Program includes a spiral-bound teacher's manual that provides a good overview of the concept of phonological awareness and directions for 21 instructional activities. In addition, it contains a selection of pictures and game boards printed on 8½ × 11 inch card stock. The kit also comes with an excellent videotape that demonstrates many of the activities in the program.

Range of Instructional Activities

The curriculum of *The Sounds Abound Program* provides instructional practice in developing rhyme, syllable, and phonemic awareness. Following most of the activities, the authors offer special instructional tips, as well as activities to provide extra instruction and practice for children who are having difficulty mastering the skill being taught. The majority of activities in this program involve singing or other musical activity. Following is a list of the specific skills taught in the program.

Rhyme

- *Recognition* (e.g., "Does *log* rhyme with *dog*?")
- *Completion* (e.g., "Jack and Jill went up the _____?")
- *Production*—Children make up rhymes for individual words (e.g., "What words rhyme with *blue*?").

Syllable Awareness

- *Segmentation*—Children count the syllables in words and pronounce the syllables separately.
- *Deletion*—Children make new words by dropping one part of a compound word (e.g., *starfish − star = fish*).

Phonemic Awareness

- *Initial Sound Recognition*—Childen select a picture beginning with a given sound, or pronounce the beginning sound of a word.

- *Phoneme Segmentation*—Children pronounce all the sounds in words; they are supported with pictures that have dots at the bottom showing the number of sounds in the words.

- *Phoneme Deletion*—Children recognize the sound that is left out when the teacher says their name after deleting the first sound (e.g., the teacher says "ark," leaving out the beginning /m/ sound).

- *Phoneme Substitution*—Children practice making "funny" words by putting different sounds at the beginning of words.

- *Phoneme Blending*—Children practice recognizing pictures or body parts when their names are pronounced one phoneme at a time (e.g., /n/-/o/-/z/, /f/-/oo/-/t/).

Activities with Letters

- *Matching Letters to First Sounds in Words*—Two activities are included that provide practice in identifying the letter that stands for the first sound in a word. The children are either given the word and must identify its first letter, or given the letter and must identify a picture that goes with it.

Research Base To Support Its Use

This program has not been evaluated in research. However, most of the activities are similar to those of other programs that have been evaluated, and that have produced significant growth in phonological awareness. The primary question about the effectiveness of this program is whether it contains enough different activities to support instruction across an entire classroom year and, thus, whether it will be as effective as those programs that include a greater variety of content and activities.

Ordering Information

The program may be obtained from LinguiSystems, Inc., 3100 4th Avenue, East Moline, IL 61244; phone: 800/776-4332.

General Comments About Use

One major strength of this program is the demonstration video that is included with the materials. It provides delightful examples of many of the activities being performed by the author with a small group of children. This video should be very useful for inservice training of teachers and for showing to parents as part of parent programs. As stated, one possible limitation of the program is the relatively small number (21) of different activities it contains; however, the manual provides suggestions for additional activities so teachers should be able to generate more practice if the children in their classes seem to require it. Finally, the program contains only two very simple activities designed to help children see the connections between sounds and letters. The program needs to be supplemented with other activities at the end to ensure that children learn to apply their newly acquired phonemic awareness to spelling and reading print.

Sounds Abound Instructional Materials and Game

Description of the Materials

The *Sounds Abound Instructional Materials and Game* (Catts & Vartiainen, 1993) has been in use in kindergarten and first-grade classrooms for a number of years. The spiral-bound book contains activities and materials to lead children from beginning rhyming activities through activities involving letters and sounds. It is written in a very simple format, and the activities are easy to implement and described concisely in the manual. It is not presented as an organized curriculum, but if teachers follow the order of activities as presented in the manual, they move gradually from easier to more difficult activities. The game is suitable for small group practice on the phonemic awareness skills introduced in the materials.

Materials Included with Purchase

The *Sounds Abound* materials are contained in a spiral-bound notebook, which contains directions for the activities and many pictures that are used with the activities. In addition, it contains a list of picture books that emphasize rhyme, song books, and fingerplay, and rhyme books that can be used to build sound awareness in young children. The manual also contains some simple tests of phonemic awareness that can be used to assess growth of these skills before and after the program is implemented. The game, which is purchased separately from the materials, contains a game board, spinner, game booklet, stimulus cards, and moving pieces.

Range of Instructional Activities

The activities in *Sounds Abound* focus on four broad areas:

Rhyme

- Activities to teach children how to judge whether or not words rhyme
- Activities that help children learn to generate rhyming words

Beginning and Ending Sounds

- Activities that teach children to make judgments about whether words begin or end with the same sound
- Activities that teach children to produce words beginning with the same sound as another word

Segmenting and Blending

- Activities that teach children to segment words into syllables
- Activities involving blending of syllables into words
- Activities that lead children to segment and pronounce the phonemes in words
- Activities that involve blending individual phonemes into words

Putting Sounds Together with Letters

- Activities that teach children the sounds associated with seven consonants and five vowels
- Structured activities in which children learn to make different words by changing the first letter (e.g., with __ at already given, the children can make *sat*, *fat*, *mat*, *pat*, and *rat* by choosing different letters)

The *Sounds Abound Game* provides practice in many of the activities introduced in the classroom materials. Specifically, it includes items that provide practice in (1) comparing beginning and ending sounds in words, (2) sound blending, and (3) sound segmenting and sound deletion.

Research Base To Support Its Use

As with most of the programs described in this guide, there is no specific research support for the *Sounds Abound* materials as a unique instructional sequence. However, all of the activities were taken directly from research projects that showed a significant impact on the growth of phonological awareness in young children.

Ordering Information

The *Sounds Abound* materials and the *Sounds Abound Game* can be ordered from LinguiSystems, Inc., 3100 4th Avenue, East Moline, IL 61244; phone: 800/776-4332.

General Comments About Use

This is an excellent set of materials for guiding phonemic awareness instruction in kindergarten or first grade. Its primary strength is the simplicity of layout, specifically the ease with which the activities can be executed in the classroom. Because there is not an elaborate game or activity structure developed for each instructional activity, the program may require a bit more creativity on the part of the teacher to maintain interest than some of the other materials described in this section. The *Sounds Abound Game* would be a useful addition to any kindergarten program in phonological awareness, and could be used by instructional aides or parent volunteers to strengthen phonological awareness in small groups of children. We recommend that the game be purchased along with the materials for maximum effectiveness and the ability to provide extra practice for those children who may require it.

Launch into Reading Success Through Phonological Awareness Training

Description of Program

Launch into Reading Success (Bennett & Ottley, 1996) was designed to provide special support in the development of phonological awareness to kindergarten children who are at risk for reading failure. Most of the activities are designed for small group rather than whole classroom instruction. The program contains 66 activity lessons that should take anywhere from 10 to 30 minutes each to complete. Because it is highly scripted, *Launch into Reading Success* can be led by teacher aides or parent volunteers, as long it is done under supervision of the classroom teacher.

Materials Included with Purchase

This program is "packaged" in a three-ring binder that contains the manual as well as all of the word lists and pictures to be used in the activities. Also included are two laminated game boards that are used in several of the activities. Some additional materials are required for a few of the activities, but these should be readily available in any kindergarten or first-grade classroom.

Range of Instructional Activities

The instructional activities for *Launch into Reading Success* are grouped within nine broad objectives. Each objective contains several instructional activities that build upon one another to achieve the desired learning outcome.

Awareness of Whole Words as Sounds—These activities focus on helping the child identify words as individual sound segments within sentences.

Tapping—The objective is to lead children to be able to tap out the number of syllables in words containing from one to four syllables.

Rhyme—This objective contains eight activities designed to lead the child from being able to recognize if two words rhyme to being able to generate rhyming words.

Onset and Rime—These five activities are designed to show how words can be broken into onset and rime segments (e.g., c-at, b-ig) and how these segments can be blended together to form words.

Segmentation—This section begins with activities to teach children how to segment words into syllables by pronouncing each syllable separately. They then learn to segment two- and three-phoneme words and pronounce the individual phonemes separately.

Discrimination—This extensive section (ll activities) develops the skill of identifying words that begin and end with the same sounds.

Pronunciation Lessons for Consonant Pairs—This section (which is more developed than similar sections in most training programs) provides instruction designed to show children the essential differences between voiced and unvoiced consonants (e.g., p–b, d–t, ch–j), and also to point out the way each of the consonant sounds are formed in the mouth.

Blending Phonemes—These five activities build skill in blending separately presented phonemes to form words.

Linkage—These 14 activities begin by teaching children to recognize the letters a, p, t, m, and i, and to associate the appropriate phonemes with them. Subsequent activities show children how these letters represent sounds in words. Most of these activities involve changing the first sounds in words by changing the letters.

Research Base To Support Its Use

This program has not been directly evaluated in research. However, its activities are similar to those contained in programs that have been shown to be effective in increasing phonological awareness. Given our experience with other, similar programs, we would expect the program to be effective with children who are mildly to moderately at risk for reading failure, and to be less effective with children who are severely at risk.

Ordering Information

Launch into Reading Success can be obtained from PRO-ED, Inc., 8700 Shoal Creek Boulevard, Austin, TX 78757-6897; phone: 800/897-3202.

General Comments About Use

This program has a number of strengths that recommend it for use with children who are at risk. First, it begins at a very basic level and moves through the steps of acquiring phonemic awareness in relatively small steps. Second, it places a strong emphasis on showing children how the sounds in words are represented in print. This may be particularly important for children who have lower ability in the phonological area. Finally, the program provides extensive practice in learning the distinct articulatory and acoustic features of individual consonant phonemes, which should help children to recognize phonemes when they occur at different positions within words. The major limitation of the program arises from the fact that it may not be sufficiently powerful to help the bottom 3% to 5% of children with the most severe phonological disabilities acquire sufficient phonological awareness to learn beginning phonetic reading skills. It also is not clear why children are taught to segment and pronounce the individual phonemes in words before they are taught how to compare words on the basis of their first and last phonemes. This latter skill is easier than full segmentation and is taught prior to segmentation in most programs.

The Lindamood Phoneme Sequencing Program for Reading, Spelling, and Speech

Description of Program

The Lindamood Phoneme Sequencing Program (LiPS) (P. Lindamood & P. Lindamood, 1998), which was formerly known as *Auditory Discrimination in Depth*, is designed to stimulate phonological awareness and teach phonemic reading skills to children with moderate to severe phonological disabilities. It is more complex than any of the other programs described in this manual, and it requires extensive teacher training to implement it successfully. It has been used for many years in clinical settings with students with severe reading disabilities, but may also be appropriate for preventive instruction with children at risk for reading disabilities.

Materials Included with Purchase

The clinical version of the LiPS program comes with a teacher's manual, a demonstration videotape, and a variety of instructional support materials, including letter tiles, mouth pictures and cards, colored blocks, and colored felt squares. The classroom version has multiple sets of materials, some of which are enlarged for whole classroom use. The manuals contain extensive descriptions of instructional procedures, as well as a complete discussion of the instructional philosophy and goals of the program. All the materials necessary for implementing the program come in the kit.

Range of Instructional Activities

The LiPS program contains instructional activities that extend all the way into fully developed phonics instruction and strategies for reading and spelling multisyllable words. Because the focus of this manual is on phonolglical awareness, our description focuses primarily on that aspect of the program.

The initial instructional activities are designed to help children become aware of the specific mouth movements associated with each phoneme in the English language. The emphasis in the LiPS program is on the "discovery" method of learning. That is, the mouth movements associated with each phoneme are not directly taught by the teacher. Rather, by asking carefully focused questions that guide the discovery process, the teacher helps the child to discover this information. Once children become aware of the mouth movements required to make a given phoneme, they learn labels for each phoneme that are descriptive of place and manner of articulation (e.g., "Lip Popper" or "Tip Tapper"), and they learn to associate each sound with a picture showing a mouth making the sound (mouth pictures). Children work initially with a small group of consonant and vowel sounds, and once they have learned the labels and mouth pictures associated with these sounds, and can explain the meaning of the labels, they engage in an extensive series of problem-solving exercises that involve representing sequences of phonemes with either mouth pictures or colored blocks. This training is designed to help them focus on mouth movements in order to "feel" the identity, number, and sequence of sounds in syllables, and it also enables them to learn to represent these sequences with concrete visual objects.

As they learn to label each phoneme with a descriptive name, they are also taught to associate specific letters with each phoneme. Thus, once children become facile at representing sequences of sounds with concrete objects, it is a natural transition to begin to represent them with letters. Children learn first to encode (spell) syllables with letters, and then to decode (read) syllables by blending the separate phonemes together. Much of this beginning work with spelling and decoding simple patterns (CV, VC, CVC combinations) includes the use of nonwords in order to reinforce the habit of "feeling" and "hearing" the individual sounds in words.

Research Base To Support Its Use

A number of recent studies support the utility of the LiPS program in teaching beginning reading skills to children with phonological disabilities. Several studies (e.g., Alexander, Anderson, Heilman, Voeller, & Torgesen, 1991; Torgesen, Wagner, Rashotte, Alexander, & Conway, 1997) have demonstrated that the program is very effective in increasing both the phonological awareness and the phonemic reading skills of older children with severe reading disabilities. There is also good evidence that the program can be used successfully with young children who are at risk for reading failure if it is offered during the initial stages of learning to read (Torgesen, Wagner, & Rashotte, 1997).

Ordering Information

The LiPS program can be obtained from PRO-ED, Inc., 8700 Shoal Creek Boulevard, Austin, TX 78757-6897; phone: 800/897-3202. A CD-ROM that contains an extensive set of practice activities in support of this program is now available through Lindamood–Bell Learning Processes. It is available by calling 800/234-6224. We would not recommend that teachers simply buy the kit and begin to use it without special training, which is offered through Lindamood–Bell Learning Processes.

General Comments About Use

LiPS is an excellent and comprehensive program for use with children who have severe difficulties acquiring phonological awareness and learning phonemic reading skills. For older children with severe reading disabilities, the typical length of treatment is about 80 hours of individual instruction, but it can sometimes range up to 160 hours. The primary limitation of the program is that it requires at least 40 hours of special teacher training in order to obtain *beginning*-level skills in its use. However, availability of the CD-ROM support may help to increase the efficiency and cost effectiveness of the program.

Phonological Awareness Training for Reading

Description of Program

The *Phonological Awareness Training for Reading* program (Torgesen & Bryant, 1993) was designed to provide small group instruction for children with weaknesses in the area of phonological awareness. It is highly scripted so that it can be followed by teachers without special training. If it is used in 30-minute sessions three times a week, it can be completed in slightly less than one semester of instruction. The program was developed with the support of a grant from the National Institute for Child Health and Human Development.

Materials Included with Purchase

Materials in the program kit include an instructors' manual, two game boards, a large picture of "Rocky the Robot" that is used during sound blending activities, six sets of laminated picture cards, a set of letter cards, several solid-color cards for use in phoneme counting activities, colored game tokens, and an audiotape that illustrates how to pronounce phonemes in isolation. All materials necessary for instruction are included in the kit.

Range of Instructional Activities

The phonological awareness skills in this program are taught and practiced using a sequence of wordsets. This structure was used so that children can become familiar with a small set of sounds by working within wordsets that contain a restricted number of phonemes. Each new wordset introduces three new consonant phonemes, for which mouth and tongue positions are explicitly taught. As the same activities are practiced across different wordsets, children's awareness skills should become more generalized.

After several sessions of warm-up activities involving rhyme, the following skills are taught with each wordset:

Set 1

- Onset/rime blending
- Phoneme blending
- Segmentation of initial phoneme

Sets 2 Through 5

- Phoneme blending
- Matching words on basis of first, last, and middle sounds
- Identifying the position of phonemes within words
- Pronouncing the first, last, and middle sounds in words

Sets 6 Through 8

- Instruction in letter–sound correspondences
- Making new words by changing the first, last, or middle letter
- Blending words when letters stand for the phonemes

Research Base To Support Its Use

Two studies have been reported that validate the effectiveness of the *Phonological Awareness Training for Reading* program. Torgesen, Morgan, and Davis (1992) found that both the segmenting and blending activities included in the program were necessary to support children's growth in the ability to read new words. Torgesen and Davis (1996) showed that the program produced a sizable *average* effect on the phonological awareness of a large group of children who were highly at risk. Overall, the skills of this group of children, which began below the 10th percentile, moved up close to average for both segmenting and blending after about 16 hours of training with the program. However, this same study also showed that a significant number of these children who were at risk did not profit significantly from the instruction, suggesting either the need for better training of the teachers or more explicit and intensive instruction.

Ordering Information

The *Phonological Awareness Training for Reading* program may be obtained from PRO-ED, Inc., 8700 Shoal Creek Boulevard, Austin, TX 78757-6897; phone: 800/897-3202.

General Comments About Use

This program is well suited for children with mild to moderate phonological awareness difficulties. It provides in-depth practice on critical phonological awareness skills, and it is paced for children with learning difficulties in this area. The program provides a strong transition into using letters to represent the sounds in words. It is relatively easy to use and requires no special training, although teachers with special training in reading or language will find it initially easier to use than those who do not have such training. Although the program was designed to help children in the second semester of kindergarten prepare for reading instruction in first grade, it can appropriately be used with children who are experiencing difficulty to read as late as the second grade.

Road to the Code: A Phonological Awareness Program for Young Children

Description of Program

Road to the Code (Blachman, Ball, Black, & Tangel, 1999) was developed over a 10-year period as part of the materials used in a set of studies on the effects of training phonemic awareness in young children. The program was finalized with support of a grant from the National Center for Learning Disabilities. It is designed to provide small group instruction to kindergarten children and children in first grade who are having trouble learning to read. Although the program is particularly well suited for children who are having special difficulties acquiring phonemic awareness, it can also be used to provide small group instruction for all children in the classroom. The program is well scripted, and it can be used by classroom teachers, resource teachers, and language specialists. If it is taught in 15- to 20-minute sessions 4 days a week, the 44 lessons of the program can be completed in approximately 11 weeks.

Materials Included with Purchase

Materials come in a loose-leaf binder that includes instructions for every activity and black-and-white line drawings for many of the materials. Some of the materials included are alphabet picture cards, sound bingo cards, Say-it-And-Move-It Sheets, and Elkonin sound cards. These materials may be photocopied, and they can be colored for added interest. Materials that are required but not included are tiles or disks for use with Say-It-And-Move-It cards, a puppet with a mouth that opens and closes, bingo chips, paper lunch bags, and other objects that are relatively easy to obtain or construct. The teacher instructions not only include scripts for the activities, but guidance about pacing and individualization of the activities in a section called "Teacher Notes."

Range of Instructional Activities

Each lesson in the *Road to the Code* contains three types of activities: the Say-It-And-Move-It activity, a lesson on letter names and sounds, and a phonological awareness practice activity.

Say-It-And-Move-It

In this activity, children show the number of sounds in words by moving tiles or disks from one area to another of the Say-It-And-Move-It sheet as they pronounce each sound. Children are introduced to this task by a set of activities in which the teacher pronounces one sound at a time, and the child simply shows the number of sounds that were pronounced by moving tiles. In Lesson 4, children are asked to begin segmenting two phoneme words, and over the next series of lessons, they acquire facility in segmenting and pronouncing the sounds in two- and three-phoneme words. By Lesson 20, most children will have learned several letter sounds, and they begin to use one or more tiles with letters on them to indicate the sounds in words that are pronounced by the teacher.

Letter Name and Sound Instruction

This *Road to the Code* activity teaches the names and sounds for eight letters (six consonants and two short vowels). The letter sounds are taught so that children can be directly taught the way that letters represent the sounds in words. Beginning with Lesson 20, children are taught to represent the sounds in words with letters, and by the end of the program, they can perform simple chaining activities (e.g., spelling *at*, then making *fat*, *mat*, *sat*, and *bat*).

Phonological Awareness Practice

This practice involves a set of varied activities ranging from identifying rhyming words to comparing words with similar beginning sounds, to sound blending activities. These activities add variety to each lesson and allow children to identify phonemes in words within a variety of contexts. Blending individual sounds into words is also practiced in these activities.

Research Base To Support Its Use

Most of the activities used in this program have been evaluated in several studies. Ball and Blachman (1991) demonstrated that the activities could produce significant improvement in the phonemic awareness of kindergarten children, and also that children who received both the phonemic awareness activities and letter–sound instruction were able to apply this training to reading words. A slightly more complete set of activities was evaluated by Blachman, Ball, Black, and Tangel (1994). In this study kindergarten teachers, rather than trained research assistants, worked with the program. This study showed that children who received the program in kindergarten were better readers at the end of Grades 1 and 2 than similar children who did not participate in phonological awareness instruction in kindergarten (Blachman, Tangel, Ball, Black, & McGraw, in press).

Ordering Information

The *Road to the Code* may be obtained from Brookes Publishing Company, P.O. Box 10624, Baltimore, MD 21285-0624; phone: 800/638-3775.

General Comments About Use

This excellent program is firmly grounded in programmatic research that has helped to refine its use with young children. A particularly strong feature of the manual is the inclusion of careful "teacher notes" that provide guidance to teachers about pacing the activities and methods for individualizing activities for children within groups. These teacher notes, as well as the very clear scripts and guidance for each of the lesson activities, should make this program easy for teachers to use effectively in their classrooms. The sequence of lessons also provides a strong transition between oral language phonemic awareness activities and the use of letters to read and spell words. With some modification of materials, many of the activities in the program could also be adapted for use with older children who continue to struggle with mastery of the alphabetic principle in reading.

DaisyQuest and Daisy's Castle

Description of the Program

DaisyQuest (Erickson, Foster, Foster, & Torgesen, 1992) and *Daisy's Castle* (Erickson, Foster, Foster, & Torgesen, 1993) are computer programs that were designed to stimulate phonemic awareness in young children. They were developed with support of a grant from the National Institute of Child Health and Human Development. Although their primary use will be with kindergarten and first-grade children, many teachers have reported using them successfully with older children receiving special education. The programs will run on almost any Macintosh computer but not on Windows or DOS. The programs use high-quality graphics and digitized speech, have an interesting story line, and are animated to hold children's interest.

Materials Included with Purchase

The programs come on several 3.5-inch disks, accompanied by a teacher's manual that provides complete instructions on how to use them. The programs come with management software that allows the teacher to specify the activities that will be available for any given child, and that also provide a report of the level of performance for each child. The program tracks the activities that have been successfully accomplished and encourages children to try new activities so that they can keep moving forward.

Range of Instructional Activities

DaisyQuest provides instruction and practice in four phonological awareness activities, and *Daisy's Castle* provides three additional activities. Each activity contains an instructional–practice module in which children are taught how to perform the activity and allowed to practice as much as they want, and two different testing modules that allow children to show what they have learned. The simplest testing module simply asks whether two words rhyme (or begin with the same first, middle, or last sound), and the second testing module requires the child to indicate which of three words rhymes (or has the same first, last, or middle sound) as a target word. As children complete different activities at a preset criterion of performance, they are rewarded with clues about where Daisy the Dragon is hiding in the world they move through in the program.

DaisyQuest Activities

- **Rhyming**—Children are taught to indicate whether or not two words rhyme.

- **First Sound Comparison**—Children learn to compare words on the basis of their first sound.

- **Last Sound Comparison**—Children compare words on the basis of last sounds.

- **Middle Sound Comparison**—Children learn to compare words on the basis of their middle sounds.

Daisy's Castle Activities

- **Onset–Rime Blending**—Children learn "two-part" blending, which involves onsets and rimes (c-at, d-og).

- **Full Blending**—Children blend all the sounds in two-, three-, and four-phoneme words to identify a specific word.

- **Counting Sounds**—Children indicate how many different sounds they hear in two-, three-, and four-phoneme words.

Research Base To Support Its Use

These computer programs have been evaluated in two studies. In the first study (Foster, Erickson, Foster, Brinkman, & Torgesen, 1994), a total of 46 children, ranging in age from 57 to 93 months, were given experience with *DaisyQuest*. With an average of approximately 9 hours of instruction, the children showed about as much improvement in phonological awareness as many teacher-led programs produce in twice that amount of time (Torgesen & Barker, 1995). Another study evaluated the use of both programs with a group of children who were experiencing reading problems after 4 months of instruction in first grade (Barker & Torgesen, 1995). The children received approximately 8 hours of instruction with both programs, and gained substantially more in phonological awareness and word reading ability than similar children who had been given experience with software to increase early reading skills or build mathematics skills.

Ordering Information

DaisyQuest and *Daisy's Castle* may be obtained from Adventure Learning Software, Inc., 965 North Eastview Drive, Alpine, UT 84004; phone: 801/756-2853.

General Comments About Use

These programs, when used together, can be helpful in providing instructional and practice activities that will stimulate phonemic awareness in young children. They can be used either as stand-alone activities or preferably as a way of providing additional experience in the context of a classroom-wide curriculum in phonological awareness. By themselves, they will probably not be sufficient to help children with severe phonological disabilities acquire useful levels of phonemic awareness. Young children of extremely low ability (this is less true for older children with reading disabilities) may require the assistance of either an older child or an instructional aide as they are introduced to different activities in the programs, because the instructional routines of these programs are not robust enough to deal with all of the learning difficulties present in children with phonological disabilities.

Earobics

Description of the Program

Earobics: Level I (Wasowicz, 1997) and *Earobics: Level II* (Wasowicz, 1999) are computer programs designed specifically to build listening skills and phonemic awareness in young children from age 4 through elementary school. The programs have a comprehensive range of activities to stimulate phonological awareness, and these activities can be engaged at many different difficulty levels (as many as 114 in Level 1 and 155 in Level 2), ranging from simple listening skills to work with letters and sounds. The graphics, quality, and program structure are high quality and should be consistently engaging for young children. The program should also be suitable for stimulating phonological awareness in older children who are experiencing delays in phonological development.

Materials Included with Purchase

Each level of *Earobics* can be purchased in two versions. The home and the Pro Plus versions are the same except that the latter version contains provision for as many as 25 children to register, whereas the home version allows only 2 children to register at a time. In addition, the Pro Plus version contains more extensive teacher control, data collection, and report writing features than the home version. Both versions come on a CD-ROM that can be played in either Macintosh or Windows environments. A small instruction booklet accompanies the CD, and there is also a Web site available to answer questions and obtain more product information (http://www.cogcon.com).

Range of Instructional Activities

All the activities in this program employ an adaptive practice format in which the level of item difficulty is adjusted according to the child's performance. The level of game difficulty is increased if the child meets a given performance criteria, and it is lowered if the items are too difficult. The goal is to allow the child to progress through items that gradually increase in difficulty until high levels of performance are obtained. Both versions of the program keep records that allow the child to resume play at the level of difficulty that was achieved in the previous session. *Earobics: Level I,* which is appropriate for children ages 4 to 7, contains six activities, each embedded in a different gamelike format. The activities can be played in any order selected by the child, or the child can focus on only a few of the activities at a time. The activities are as follows:

- **Karloon's Balloons**—This activity strengthens listening skills by requiring the child to remember sequences of sound effects, words, numbers, or speech sounds. The computer provides an auditory sequence, and the child must then click on pictures associated with the sounds in the right order. There are 38 levels of play for this activity.

- **C.C. Coal Car**—This activity teaches letter–sound correspondence and phonemic awareness. Across 74 levels of play, the child begins by simply indicating whether a given phoneme matches a letter, and ends with levels that require the child to indicate where a given sound occurs within a three-phoneme word.

- **Rap-A-Tap-Tap**—This activity teaches phonemic segmentation across 16 levels of play. The child begins by simply counting the number of separate drum beats in a given sequence, and it ends with items that involve counting the number of syllables or phonemes in words.

- **Caterpillar Connection**—This phoneme-blending activity begins with blending compound words and ends with blending phonemes. There are 56 levels of play.

- **Rhyme Time**—This activity, which contains 11 levels of play, teaches children to identify words that rhyme.

- **Basket Full of Eggs**—This activity begins by helping children learn to hear the differences between vowels, and between consonant–vowel combinations. The computer pronounces two vowels, or combinations, and the child simply indicates if they are the same or different. When the child is working with consonant–vowel combinations, the early levels of difficulty acoustically enhance the distinctiveness of the combinations, and this distinctiveness is gradually reduced as the child moves through the program. There are 114 levels of play in this activity.

Earobics: Level II, which is designed for children ages 7 through 10, has five activities that provide additional support for the development of phonemic awareness and letter knowledge:

- **Calling All Engines**—This program, which has 168 levels of difficulty, requires children to recall increasingly complex sequences of auditory and verbal information. It also introduces increasingly complex directions that must be remembered and interpreted.

- **Paint by Penguin**—Easy levels of this activity involve counting the number of sounds in a sequence, and the game progresses until the child is counting the number of sounds in complex syllables, and rearranging phonemes to form new words. This activity has 68 levels of difficulty.

- **Pesky Parrots**—This game provides practice in blending sounds to form words. It begins with syllable blending and moves to blending of phonemes in complex syllables. It has 60 levels of difficulty.

- **Hippo Hoops**—This activity, which has 155 levels of play, begins by requiring simple discriminations between the sounds in words, and ends by requiring children to indicate the position of a specific sound in a word that is represented by a letter or letters on the screen.

- **Duck Luck**—This activity begins by asking the child to indicate which of several spoken words contains a given sound (represented by a letter) in the initial or final position. It advances to activities requiring children to indicate what word remains when a given sound is removed from another word. The activity has 142 levels of difficulty.

Research Base To Support Its Use

We are not aware of any published research that documents the effectiveness of this program. However, the activities themselves, and the levels of difficulty for each activity, are consistent with principles of effective instruction in phonemic awareness. If this program is used consistently with young children, it should have similar effects as other instructional programs that follow the same principles. Given the large range of difficulty of the items in *Earobics*, the program appears to have special potential to enhance phonemic awareness in children with phonological processing difficulties.

Ordering Information

Earobics can be ordered from Cognitive Concepts, Inc., 207 Hamilton Street, Evanston, IL 60202; phone: 847/328-8199. More information about the products can be obtained at the Web site for Cognitive Concepts (http://www.cogcon.com).

General Comments About Use

Earobics has a number of important strengths that recommend its use both at home and in the schools. The activities in the program follow principles of good instruction in phonemic awareness, and they are provided at many levels of difficulty to support gradual growth and extra practice for children who have difficulty in this area. The program's most obvious limitation is that the format of feedback, and of the games themselves, may become repetitious for children who spend a lot of time with the program. For children who have difficulty learning in this area, teachers and parents may have to structure additional rewards for progress through increasingly challenging levels of the program. The program should provide excellent supplemental instruction to kindergarten and first-grade children who are receiving classroom-level instruction in phonemic awareness but are having difficulty keeping up with their peers.

Read, Write, and Type

Description of the Program

Read, Write, and Type (Herron, 1995) is a computer program designed to teach children to read through writing. It is included in this manual because it contains many activities that are explicitly designed to build phonemic awareness, and initial research suggests that it can be used effectively to help children with phonological weaknesses acquire beginning reading skills. It uses the full multimedia capabilities of modern computers to provide engaging instructional and practice activities for young children. It can be used with whole classroom groups to teach typing and writing skills, or it can be used more intensively with children who are at risk to teach these same skills plus reading.

Materials Included with Purchase

The *Read, Write, and Type* program can be ordered in at least two versions. The version for teachers includes the program on a CD-ROM plus a teacher's manual that describes a variety of learning activities to be used prior to introducing students to the same content on the computer. These teacher-led activities are designed to help make the computer-based learning and practice experience more successful for young children. The manual also contains many pictures and word lists that can be copied and used in teacher-led instructional activities. The home version of the program does not include the instructional manual.

Range of Instructional Activities

Read, Write, and Type contains 40 lessons, each of which is designed to introduce a new phoneme and provide practice hearing it in words, as well as typing it by itself, and in words and stories. One of the major instructional goals of this program is to provide children with the skills necessary to type any regularly spelled word they hear. It brings meaning to this task by engaging children in writing and reading tasks at the sentence and story levels. Within the context of this program, children primarily read material that they themselves have typed. Thus, it is not a stand-alone reading program, but rather is designed to provide a meaningful context for teaching phonemic awareness and phonetic writing and reading skills. A few simple phonics rules, such as the signal 'e' (which makes the middle vowel say its name), are taught in the teacher-led lessons accompanying the program.

Each lesson provides the following experiences with each of the 40 phonemes and letter–sound correspondences taught by the program:

1. **Initial Instruction in How To Type the Sound**—This includes direct instruction and modeling by animated "hands," as well as practice typing the phoneme in words and short phrases.

2. **Phonemic Awareness**—This activity provides practice in "listening" for the sound within words. The child is shown a picture and must indicate whether the given phoneme occurs at the beginning, middle, or end of the word.

3. **Practicing the Phoneme in the Context of a Story**—This activity requires the child to type a simple story that is dictated by the computer, and which is spelled using words and phonemes the child should know. There is substantial visual support and prompting to help children with this task.

In addition to these standard activities for each phoneme, areas in the program encourage the improvement of fluency in typing and creative writing in the form of email messages. The program monitors child progress and provides certificates for the completion of each level of instruction.

Research Base To Support Its Use

The *Read, Write, and Type* program has been evaluated in both whole classroom and small group instructional applications. With whole classroom groups, it is typically used for 45 minutes a day, with part of that time being teacher-led instruction. Initial reports (J. Herron, personal communication, July 1997) of this use of the program are encouraging, with most children in first and second grades being able to acquire useful typing skills and improving in their ability to spell and apply phonetic reading skills during reading. In another study (Torgesen, Wagner, & Rashotte, 1998), the program was used with small groups of three children who were at risk in four 50-minute sessions a week for 8 months of the school year. Although these children began the year with reading skills substantially below their peers, their scores on phonetic reading ability, sight word reading, and passage comprehension were all average to slightly above average at the end of the year. Also, almost all of the children learned useful typing skills from the program.

Ordering Information

The *Read, Write, and Type* program is available from the Learning Company, 6160 Summit Drive North, Minneapolis, MN 55430; phone: 800/152-2255.

General Comments About Use

This is a well-designed and executed program, with engaging graphics and sound. Children enjoy working on the program for extended periods of time. The instructions and activities in the teacher's manual are also instructionally sound, and fun for both teachers and children. The program is not recommended as a stand-alone experience for children who are at risk, but, with teacher support, it appears to be a very effective way to prevent reading problems in these children in first grade. For children with more normal learning abilities in reading, the program provides a helpful additional experience to stimulate writing skills and learning to type.

Waterford Early Reading Program—Level 1

Description of the Program

The *Waterford Early Reading Program—Level 1* (Waterford Institute, 1993) provides a rich set of instructional and practice experiences focused on pre-reading knowledge and skills. It took 5 years and $7 million dollars to develop, and its development has been supported through grants from a variety of foundations. It represents an attempt to use computers to teach all the major skills and knowledge involved in learning to read. The instruction takes advantage of the full multimedia capabilities of our most advanced personal computers and includes original songs, art work, full-motion video, and animation. These activities have been designed to capture and hold the attention of young children. Level 1 is followed by Levels 2 and 3 in the first and second grades, respectively. The Level 1 curriculum for kindergarten children provides approximately 15 to 20 minutes of daily instruction to extend over the entire school year.

Materials Included with Purchase

The Waterford curriculum is by far the most expensive instructional package described in this manual. It is sold in units that support instruction for an entire classroom, and each unit typically includes three high-end multimedia computers, teacher's manuals that describe supportive classroom activities, and materials, including 40 individual readers and four videotapes for each child to take home.

Range of Instructional Activities

The instructional objectives of the Level 1 curriculum fall into six categories:

1. **Print Awareness**—Activities within this objective teach such things as learning letter names and sounds, understanding direction of print, and writing and forming letters and words.

2. **Phonological Skills**—This component focuses directly on phonological awareness. Children receive extensive experience with rhyme; matching words on first, middle, and last sounds; phoneme blending; and counting the sounds in words.

3. **Visual Perception**—This segment teaches children to recognize shapes, patterns, and details in visual material.

4. **Listening Skills**—These activities help children to hone their listening skills with music and aurally presented stories.

5. **Concept Development**—This component focuses on such things as learning about numbers, opposites, story sequence, making predictions in stories, and distinguishing between real and make-believe.

6. **Computer Skills**—Children learn to use a mouse and practice beginning keyboard skills.

The activities in each component are varied from day to day and build in a sequence from simpler to more difficult activities. The program keeps track of children's progress and automatically provides the instruction their development warrants.

Research Base To Support Its Use

The Level 1 curriculum has been evaluated at numerous sites around the country, including large city urban schools, suburban schools, and rural schools. The addition of the computer experiences to the standard kindergarten curriculum has consistently produced large gains in prereading skills at the end of the year. Measures have included tests of phonological awareness, letter knowledge, and concepts about print. The major unknown at present about this curriculum is whether it will prove to be more effective than less costly teacher-led interventions. No studies are currently available to indicate that it will produce larger gains in prereading skills than might be obtained through teacher training in a kindergarten curriculum focusing on the same skills. However, this may not be the crucial question. The Waterford Curriculum is a standard curriculum that will remain in place even if trained teachers move away from a school, or if district policies about teacher training and support change. The most important question is whether a high-quality computer-based curriculum will provide more long-term stability for appropriate and effective instruction than will the less costly materials that depend on teacher training and support to implement effectively.

Ordering Information

Addison Wesley has established a new branch of their company (Electronic Education) to handle marketing for the *Waterford Early Reading Program*. This program should not simply be "ordered" as most of the curriculum materials in this manual can be, but rather school district personnel should consult the local state sales representative about purchasing the materials. The cost of the program will vary with the components that are ordered. More information about the program may be obtained by calling 888/977-7900.

General Comments About Use

The Waterford Program is the most comprehensive, highest quality computer-based curriculum in essential prereading skills currently available. Evidence suggests that it is effective in teaching phonological awareness and other important skills necessary for early reading growth. It does not require extensive teacher training to implement, although its overall effectiveness might be significantly enhanced if teachers were more carefully trained to use the supplemental materials provided within the program.

REFERENCES

Adams, M., Foorman, B., Lundberg, I., & Beeler, C. (1997). *Phonemic awareness in young children: A classroom curriculum.* Baltimore: Brookes.

Alexander, A., Anderson, H., Heilman, P. C., Voeller, K. S., & Torgesen, J. K. (1991). Phonological awareness training and remediation of analytic decoding deficits in a group of severe dyslexics. *Annals of Dyslexia, 41,* 193–206.

Ball, E. W., & Blachman, B. A. (1991). Does phoneme awareness training in kindergarten make a difference in early word recognition and developmental spelling? *Reading Research Quarterly, 26,* 49–66.

Barker, T. A., & Torgesen, J. K. (1995). An evaluation of computer-assisted instruction in phonological awareness with below average readers. *Journal of Educational Computing Research, 13,* 89–103.

Beck, I. L., & Juel, C. (1995). The role of decoding in learning to read. *American Educator, 19,* 8–42.

Bennett, L., & Ottley, P. (1996). *Launch into reading success through phonological awareness training.* Austin, TX: PRO-ED.

Blachman, B. A. (1997). Early intervention and phonological awareness: A cautionary tale. In B. Blachman (Ed.), *Foundations of reading acquisition and dyslexia: Implications for early intervention* (pp. 409–430). Mahwah, NJ: Erlbaum.

Blachman, B., Ball, E., Black, S., & Tangel, D. (1994). Kindergarten teachers develop phoneme awareness in low-income, inner-city classrooms: Does it make a difference? *Reading and Writing: An Interdisciplinary Journal, 6,* 1–17.

Blachman, B. A., Ball, E. W., Black, R. S., & Tangel, D. M. (1999). *Road to the code: A phonological awareness program for young children.* Baltimore: Brookes.

Blachman, B. A., Tangel, D. M., Ball, E. W., Black, R. S., & McGraw, C. (in press). Developing phonological awareness and word recognition skills: A two-year intervention with low-income, inner-city children. *Reading and Writing: An Interdisciplinary Journal.*

Bradley, L., & Bryant, P. (1985). *Rhyme and reason in reading and spelling.* Ann Arbor: University of Michigan Press.

Bryant, P., MacLean, M., Bradley, L., & Crossland, J. (1990). Rhyme and alliteration, phoneme detection and learning to read. *Developmental Psychology, 26,* 429–438.

Catts, H., & Vartianen, T. (1993). *Sounds abound: Listening, rhyming, and reading.* East Moline, IL: LinguiSystems.

Comprehensive Test of Basic Skills. (1974). Monterey, CA: McGraw-Hill.

Ehri, L. C. (1998). Grapheme–phoneme knowledge is essential for learning to read words in English. In J. Metsala & L. Ehri (Eds.), *Word recognition in beginning reading* (pp. 3–40). Hillsdale, NJ: Erlbaum.

Erickson, G. C., Foster, K. C., Foster, D. F., & Torgesen, J. K. (1992). *DaisyQuest.* Scotts Valley, CA: Great Wave Software.

Erickson, G. C., Foster, K. C., Foster, D. F., & Torgesen, J. K. (1993). *Daisy's Castle*. Scotts Valley, CA: Great Wave Software.

Fletcher, J. M., Shaywitz, S. E., Shankweiler, D. P., Katz, L., Liberman, I. Y., Stuebing, K. K., Francis, D. J., Fowler, A. E., & Shaywitz, B. A. (1994). Cognitive profiles of reading disability: Comparisons of discrepancy and low acheivement definitions. *Journal of Educational Psychology, 86*, 6–23.

Foorman, B. R., Francis, D. J., Fletcher, J. M., Schatschneider, C., & Mehta, P. (1998). The role of instruction in learning to read: Preventing reading failure in at-risk children. *Journal of Educational Psychology, 90*, 37–55.

Foorman, B. R., Francis, D. J., Shaywitz, S. E., Shaywitz, S. E., & Fletcher, J. M. (1996). The case for early reading intervention. In B. A. Blachman (Ed.), *Foundations of reading acquisition and dyslexia: Implications for early intervention* (pp. 243–264). Mahwah, NJ: Erlbaum.

Foster, K. C., Erickson, G. C., Foster, D. F., Brinkman, D., & Torgesen, J. K. (1994). Computer administered instruction in phonological awareness: Evaluation of the *DaisyQuest* program. *Journal of Research and Development in Education, 27*, 126–137.

Herron, J. (1995). *Read, write, and type*. Minneapolis: The Learning Co.

Hoien, T., Lundberg, I., Stanovich, K. E., & Bjaalid, I. (1995). Components of phonological awareness. *Reading and Writing: An Interdisciplinary Journal, 7*, 171–188.

Jastak, J. F., & Jastak, S. (1978). *The Wide Range Achievement Test–Revised*. Wilmington, DE: Jastak Associates.

Lenchner, O., & Podhajski, B. (1997). *The sounds abound program: Teaching phonological awareness in the classroom*. East Moline, IL: LinguiSystems.

Liberman, I. Y., Shankweiler, D., & Liberman, A. M. (1989). The alphabetic principle and learning to read. In D. Shankweiler & I. Y. Liberman (Eds.), *Phonology and reading disability: Solving the reading puzzle* (pp. 1–33). Ann Arbor: University of Michigan Press.

Lindamood, C. H., & Lindamood, P. C. (1979). *Lindamood Auditory Conceptualization Test*. Austin, TX: PRO-ED.

Lindamood, P., & Lindamood, P. (1998). *The Lindamood phoneme sequencing program for reading, spelling, and speech*. Austin, TX: PRO-ED.

Lonigan, C. J., Burgess, S. R., Anthony, J. L., & Barker, T. A. (1998). Development of phonological sensitivity in two- to five-year-old children. *Journal of Educational Psychology, 90*, 294–311.

Lundberg, I., Frost, J., & Peterson, O. (1988). Effects of an extensive program for stimulating phonological awareness in pre-school children. *Reading Research Quarterly, 23*, 263–284.

Mann, V. A. (1993). Phoneme awareness and future reading ability. *Journal of Learning Disabilities, 4*, 259–269.

Mann, V. A., Tobin, P., & Wilson, R. (1987). Measuring phonological awareness through the invented spellings of kindergarten children. *Merrill-Palmer Quarterly, 33*, 365–389.

Notari-Syverson, A., O'Connor, R. E., & Vadasy, P. F. (1998). *Ladders to literacy: A preschool activity book*. Baltimore: Brookes.

O'Connor, R. A., Jenkins, J. R., & Slocum, T. A. (1995). Transfer among phonological tasks in kindergarten: Essential instructional content. *Journal of Educational Psychology, 2*, 202–217.

O'Connor, R. A., Notari-Syverson, A., & Vadasy, P. F. (1996). Ladders to literacy: The effects of teacher-led phonological activities for kindergarten children with and without disabilities. *Exceptional Children, 63*, 117–130.

O'Connor, R. E., Notari-Syverson, A., & Vadasy, P. F. (1998). *Ladders to literacy: A kindergarten activity book*. Baltimore: Brookes.

Olson, R., Forsberg, H., Wise, B., & Rack, J. (1994). Measurement of word recognition, orthographic, and phonological skills. In G. R. Lyon (Ed.), *Frames of reference for the assessment of learning disabilities* (pp. 243–277). Baltimore: Brookes.

Robertson, C., & Salter, W. (1997). *The Phonological Awareness Test*. East Moline, IL: LinguiSystems.

Rosner, J. (1975). *Helping children overcome learning disabilities*. New York: Walker & Co.

Rosner, J. (1993). *Helping children overcome learning disabilities* (3rd ed.). New York: Walker & Co.

Sawyer, D. J. (1987). *Test of Awareness of Language Segments*. Rockville, MD: Aspen.

Share, D. L., & Stanovich, K. E. (1995). Cognitive processes in early reading development: A model of acquisition and individual differences. *Issues in Education: Contributions from Educational Psychology, 1*, 1–57.

Slocum, T. A., O'Connor, R. E., & Jenkins, J. R. (1993). Transfer among phonological manipulation skills. *Journal of Educational Psychology, 85*, 618–630.

Stanovich, K. E., Cunningham, A. E., & Cramer, B. B. (1984). Assessing phonological awareness in kindergarten children: Issues of task comparability. *Journal of Experimental Child Psychology, 38*, 175–190.

Torgesen, J. K. (in press). Individual differences in response to early interventions in reading: The lingering problem of treatment resisters. *Learning Disabilities Research and Practice*.

Torgesen, J. K., & Barker, T. (1995). Computers as aids in the prevention and remediation of reading disabilities. *Learning Disabilities Quarterly, 18*, 76–88.

Torgesen, J. K., & Bryant, B. R. (1993). *Phonological awareness training for reading*. Austin, TX: PRO-ED.

Torgesen, J. K., & Bryant, B. (1994). *Test of Phonological Awareness*. Austin, TX. PRO-ED.

Torgesen, J. K., Bryant, B. R., Wagner, R. K., & Pearson, N. (1992). Toward development of a kindergarten group test for phonological awareness. *Journal of Research and Development in Education, 25*, 111–120.

Torgesen, J. K., & Davis, C. (1996). Individual difference variables that predict response to training in phonological awareness. *Journal of Experimental Child Psychology, 63*, 1–21.

Torgesen, J. K., Morgan, S. T., & Davis, C. (1992). Effects of two types of phonological awareness training on word learning in kindergarten children. *Journal of Educational Psychology, 84*, 364–370.

Torgesen, J. K., & Wagner, R. K. (1999). Alternative diagnostic approaches for specific developmental reading disabilities. *Learning Disabilities Research and Practice, 13*, 220–232.

Torgesen, J. K., Wagner, R. K., & Rashotte, C. A. (1994). Longitudinal studies of phonological processing and reading. *Journal of Learning Disabilities, 27*, 276–286.

Torgesen, J. K., Wagner, R. K., & Rashotte, C. A. (1997). The prevention and remediation of severe reading disabilities: Keeping the end in mind. *Scientific Studies of Reading, 1*, 217–234.

Torgesen, J. K., Wagner, R. K., & Rashotte, C. A. (1998, September). *The prevention and remediation of reading disabilities: Intervention research at FSU*. Paper presented at the National Institute of Child Health and Human Development's Conference on Interventions in Reading, Bethesda, MD.

Torgesen, J. K., Wagner, R. K., Rashotte, C. A., Alexander, A. W., & Conway, T. (1997). Preventive and remedial interventions for children with severe reading disabilities. *Learning Disabilities: An Interdisciplinary Journal, 8*, 51–62.

Wagner, R. K., Torgesen, J. K., Laughon, P., Simmons, K., & Rashotte, C. A. (1993). The development of young readers' phonological processing abilities. *Journal of Educational Psychology, 85,* 1–20.

Wagner, R. K., Torgesen, J. K., & Rashotte, C. A. (1994). The development of reading-related phonological processing abilities: New evidence of bi-directional causality from a latent variable longitudinal study. *Developmental Psychology, 30,* 73–87.

Wagner, R. K., Torgesen, J. K., & Rashotte, C. A. (1999). *Comprehensive Test of Phonological Processes.* Austin, TX: PRO-ED.

Wagner, R. K., Torgesen, J. K., Rashotte, C. A., Hecht, S. A., Barker, T. A., Burgess, S. R., Donahue, J., & Garon, T. (1997). Changing causal relations between phonological processing abilities and word-level reading as children develop from beginning to skilled readers: A 5-year longitudinal study. *Developmental Psychology, 33,* 468–479.

Wasowicz, J. (1997). *Earobics: Level I.* Evanston, IL: Cognitive Concepts.

Wasowicz, J. (1999). *Earobics: Level II.* Evanston, IL: Cognitive Concepts.

Waterford Institute. (1993). *Waterford Early Reading Program—Level 1.* Menlo Park, CA: Addison Wesley.

Wharton-McDonald, R., Pressley, M., & Hampston, J. M. (1998). Literacy instruction in nine first-grade classrooms: Teacher characteristics and student achievement. *The Elementary School Journal, 99,* 101–128.

Whitehurst, G. J., & Lonigan, C. J. (1998). Child development and emergent literacy. *Child Development, 69,* 848–872.

Woodcock, R. W. (1987). *Woodcock Reading Mastery Tests–Revised.* Circle Pines, MN: American Guidance Service.

Yopp, H. K. (1988). The validity and reliability of phonemic awareness tests. *Reading Research Quarterly, 23,* 159–177.

Yopp, H. K. (1995). A test for assessing phonemic awareness in young children. *The Reading Teacher, 49,* 20–29.